CHRISTMAS READINGS TO RECAPTURE THE WONDER OF THE SEASON

CHRISTMAS
READINGS TO RECAPTURE THE WONDER OF THE SEASON

Harold Shaw Publishers
Wheaton, Illinois

ISBN 0-87788-131-6

Cover and inside design © 1995 by David LaPlaca

Compiled by Sanna Anderson Baker and Mary Horner

Library of Congress Cataloging-in-Publication Data

Christmas readings to recapture the wonder of the season / [compiled by]
Sanna Anderson Baker and Mary Horner.
p. cm.
ISBN 0-87788-131-6
1. Christmas—Literary collections. I. Baker, Sanna Anderson. II. Horner, Mary.
PN6071.C6C5586 1995
808.8′033—dc20 95-30249
CIP

---

02 01 00 99 98 97 96 95

10 9 8 7 6 5 4 3 2 1

To Sanna Anderson Baker

With grateful appreciation
for her help in shaping the direction of this book
and uncovering many of the delightful stories and poems included.
Her knowledge of children's literature
has marked this volume with a unique variety and richness,
and her life has modeled a courageous,
childlike trust in the Christ of Christmas.

Contents

Expectation

Wonder

Joy

HOPE

Grateful acknowledgment is made to the following for permission to reprint their works:

"Angels and Other Strangers," taken from *Angels and Other Strangers: Family Christmas Stories,* © 1979 by Katherine Paterson. Reprinted by permission of HarperCollins Publishers.

"Away in a Manger," © 1993 by Jon Peterson. Reprinted by permission of author.

"Born to Raise the Sons of Earth," © 1986 by Mark Noll. Reprinted by permission of author.

"Child," © 1981 by Elizabeth Rooney. Reprinted by permission of author.

"The Elm School Christmas Play," taken from *Collected Shorter Poems,* © 1988 by Nelson Bentley. Reprinted by permission of Bellowing Ark Press.

"A Night the Stars Danced for Joy," taken from *Angels, Angels All Around,* © 1993 by Bob Hartman. Reprinted by permission of Lion Publishing.

"Paperwhites," © 1993 by Sanna Anderson Baker. Reprinted by permission of author.

Luke 2:8-20, taken from the Phillips' Translation from the *New Testament in Modern English,* revised edition, © 1958, 1960, 1972 by J. B. Phillips. Reprinted by permission of the Macmillan Publishing Company, Inc.

Introduction

It is good to be children sometimes, and never better than at Christmas, when its mighty Founder was a child himself.—Charles Dickens

Christmas is a magical time when anticipating good things leaves one sleepless; when believing in the impossible with wide-eyed wonder is the most rational thing in the world; when giving from the heart is a joyous thing to do; when remembering the Child of Christmas yields the best hope of life. Perhaps at no other time of the year do we have the delight and luxury of becoming childlike again, reveling in the mystery of the season.

All too often the beauty and meaning of Christmas can be displaced by a hurried cynicism, and we forget the wonder of it all. But the miracle of Christmas is that it never grows old. Phillips Brooks observed that "the earth has grown old with its burden of care, but at Christmas it always is young." This collection is designed to help you grow young again—to see Christmas through the eyes of a child.

Included are a wide variety of stories and poems for children and adults, some written over a hundred years ago, some written in the last ten years. Though representing different time periods, each piece reflects an aspect of the expectation, wonder, joy, and hope that the Christmas season holds. As you read aloud to your family or enjoy reading alone, may the timeless characters and themes in these works restore some of the wonder of Christmas to your life, and enable you to see anew the Child whose birth we celebrate.

EXPECTATION

Good news: but if you ask me what it is, I know not;
It is a track of feet in the snow,
It is a lantern showing a path,
It is a door set open.

G. K. CHESTERTON

Christmas Everywhere

PHILLIPS BROOKS
(1835–1893)

Everywhere, everywhere, Christmas tonight!
Christmas in lands of the fir-tree and pine,
Christmas in lands of the palm-tree and vine,
Christmas where snow peaks stand solemn and white,
Christmas where corn fields stand sunny and bright.

Christmas where children are hopeful and gay,
Christmas where old men are patient and gray,
Christmas where peace, like a dove in his flight,
Broods o'er brave men in the thick of the fight;
Everywhere, everywhere, Christmas tonight!

ANGELS AND OTHER STRANGERS

KATHERINE PATERSON
(1932–)

Minutes after the letter came from Arlene, Jacob set out walking for Washington. He wondered how long it would take him to get there. Before the truck died, he could make it in an hour, but he'd never tried to walk it. At sixty he knew that he didn't have the endurance that he had once had, but he was still a strong man. Perhaps he could get there by morning if he kept a steady pace. Or if he could at least reach a place where there was a bus, he could ride as far as the few bills in his pocket could take him.

Arlene needed him, so he would go to her if he had to walk every step of the way. Arlene, his baby granddaughter, whom it seemed as if he had only just stopped bouncing on his knee, was going to have a baby herself. She was alone and scared in the city and wanted her granddaddy, so he had put on his dead wife's overcoat and then his own and started out. The two coats protected him from the wet snow, but his wife's was too small and cut under his arms. "I'm coming, Arlene baby," he said to the country road. "I'm going to be with you for Christmas."

How wonderful it would be, thought Jacob, if someone stopped and offered him a ride. Occasionally a car would pass, even on this almost deserted stretch. Once he almost raised his arm to try to wave one down, but thought better of it. Who would give a ride to a black man on a lonely road? He could hope in the Lord, but he'd better rely on his own two feet. No rest, as the Good Book said, for the weary.

In Washington, Julia Thompson was humming as she worked. Why was she so happy? Because she had two beautiful children and a loving husband. Because Walter, her husband, would be singing at the Christmas Eve service, and she always felt so proud and was thrilled by his voice. Because it was nearly Christmas. Yes, of course, all those things, but, hallelujah, it was the first Christmas since she'd known Walter that she hadn't had to deal with his Aunt Patty.

Aunt Patty was Walter's only living relative. Some respect was due her for his sake, but nothing ever went quite right with Aunt Patty. The best years were the ones when she had simply grumbled her way through the celebration, taking the edge off everyone else's enjoyment. But the last three years, she'd managed to orchestrate a series of disasters, though how could you blame an old lady for falling down on the church walk just before Christmas Eve service and having to be rushed to the hospital with a broken hip? Perhaps Aunt Patty should have known enough not to give a two-year-old a teddy bear with button eyes which he could and would immediately pull out and swallow, but she had not known, and it had meant that they had spent Christmas Day with Kevin in the emergency room. Last year, despite Julia's apprehension, everything had gone well, until they, with great excitement, told her the news that they were expecting another child. Aunt Patty, who had never before revealed a social conscience, suddenly burst into a lament for all the starving people in the world. Here they were, gorging themselves and daring to be happy, while at the same time producing still another baby to crowd out the hungry millions.

But this year, despite Walter's urgings, Aunt Patty had decided not to make the thirty-mile trip into the city. The weather was uncertain, and her bursitis had been acting up. Julia cleaned the house and shopped and baked with an energy she hadn't possessed since before Jenny was born. She even had strength left over to take the children on long walks and read aloud to Kevin. It was going to be a wonderful Christmas.

Julia put the baby down for a nap and then took Kevin up on her own bed and began reading to him. Ordinarily, Kevin loved being read to, but today he squirmed and wriggled straight through "The Night Before Christmas."

"My, you're fidgety," she said.

"Little boys are supposed to be fidgety," he said with dignity.

She hugged him close. "Now this is the story from the Bible about when Jesus was born. Try to listen, all right?"

"All right."

She read him the story of Mary and Joseph coming down from Nazareth to Bethlehem, stopping to explain about the taxes, the crowded inn, and the manger, going on to the shepherds in the field.

" 'And, lo, the angel of the Lord came upon them, and the glory of the Lord'—well, it's like a great light, Kevin—'shone round about them: and they were sore afraid. And the angel said unto them, Fear not . . . ' "

"Why were they afraid, Mommy?"

"I don't know—I guess the light and the strangeness. They'd never seen a real angel before."

He seemed satisfied. She read on, and since he was beginning to nod, she finished the whole chapter in a quiet voice until he was sound asleep. Julia propped pillows around him and went into the kitchen to clean up the lunch things and get ready for the evening. It was then that she discovered that they had no tangerines. Perhaps she was being silly, Kevin was only four and Jenny scarcely five months, but a Christmas stocking without a tangerine in the toe seemed somehow incomplete, and Julia was determined that this be a perfect Christmas. She got Becky the teen-ager from next door to baby-sit long enough to let her drive to the grocery store to pick up a few. She was home within twenty minutes.

"Everything quiet?" she asked the sitter.

"Sure. Fine. Your aunt called."

Julia's heart sank. "She said to tell you she'd changed her mind and would Mr. Thompson please come pick her up."

Julia should have asked Becky to stay with the children and gone then and there to get Aunt Patty, but she didn't. She paid Becky a dollar and sent her home before she tried to figure out what to do. Could she pretend she never got the message? No. She dialed Walter's office, looking at her watch as she did so. It was now three thirty. If he could leave Washington right away, he could drive the thirty-odd miles to Bethel, pick up Aunt Patty, and get back in time for his rehearsal. But when his secretary finally answered, it was to say that there had been an accident in the plant in Virginia, and that Walter had gone out to see about it. If he called in, she would have him call home.

That settled it. It was too late. There was no way to get Aunt Patty today, unless— Reluctantly she dialed the neighbors. No, Becky had already gone out with friends. She'd tried, Julia told herself. She really had. No one would expect her to put two sleeping children in the car and drive halfway across Maryland in bad weather.

The phone rang. "Julia?" It was, of course, Aunt Patty. "I want you just to forget my message. You mustn't bother Walter about me at such a busy time. It looks like snow anyhow. It would be ridiculous to come all the way out here."

Kevin came padding down the hall in his sock feet. "Who's that, Mommy?" he asked, still half asleep.

"Aunt Patty," Julia said.

"Aunt Patty!" His face lit up. "She's coming for Christmas!"

"Now I don't want you to feel bad," Aunt Patty was saying. "Just forget all about me and have a wonderful—"

"Aunt Patty," Julia broke in wearily, "we'll be there to get you as soon as we can."

There was a silence at the other end of the line. "Well, I think it's ridiculous to try to make it out here in this weather, but. . . . Well, all right. Since you insist."

Julia woke the baby and bundled both children into the car. It was already getting dark and snowing lightly, but she couldn't honestly say that the roads were dangerous. Even driving slowly, she should have plenty of time to get out to Aunt Patty's house in the country and back in time for the service. Of course she hadn't counted on the crowded interstate on Christmas Eve afternoon. They alternately crawled and sat, motors idling, horns honking about them.

On the back seat Jenny slept while Kevin chattered away. He was so excited about getting his Aunt Patty that he sang songs about it, substituting Aunt Patty for Santa Claus. I ought to deserve some credit, Julia thought, that despite everything, I've never turned Kevin against her.

It was nearly five before they were off the main highway and moving at a decent rate of speed. If the visibility had been really poor or the road icy, Julia would have turned around for home even then. But there was no way she could escape this journey now without disappointing her little boy and making herself feel like Scrooge incarnate.

They were dangerously low on gas, but there was a station just this side of Aunt Patty's place where she could fill up, so she pushed on. When they got there, though, the station was closed for the holiday, so she drove on to Aunt Patty's house.

"Just wait with Jenny, Kevin. I'll run in and get Aunt Patty, and we'll be right back." She dashed from the driveway to the back door and banged. It was bitter cold, though the snow was slackening. She tried the door. It fell open. "Aunt Patty?" she called in the hallway. One of Aunt Patty's cats came bouncing down the steps, meowing menacingly. "Aunt Patty?" She was seized with a sudden panic that the old woman might be lying somewhere in the house, ill or worse. Then her eye fell on the note on the kitchen table.

"Walter," it said. "I've just run up to Gertrude's for a minute. You can pick me up there or wait here for me. I won't be long. Love." Walter, were he here, might know who Gertrude was, but Julia had no notion. She wouldn't even know how to look her up in the phone book.

She went back to the car.

"Where's Aunt Patty?" asked Kevin. Where indeed was Aunt Patty?

"She went to see a friend and is coming back soon. We'll go put some gas in the car. By the time we get back, she'll probably be here."

"Why'd she go away? Didn't she know we were coming?"

Julia started the engine and began backing down the drive. She was not going to ruin Christmas by losing her temper.

"Why, Mommy?"

"I don't know, Kevin. She didn't tell me."

"Did you see her?"

"No. She left a note." Addressed to Walter, naturally.

"What did the note say?"

"She just said she was going out for a few minutes and would be right back."

"Why?"

"Kevin!"

"Why'd you yell at me, Mommy?"

"Please, Kevin. I've got to watch the road." Where in the world was the nearest gas station? One that would still be open at five thirty on Christmas Eve? There was a housing development with a shopping center somewhere about—she had driven there once with Walter—if she could remember the road to take to cut over to it. Aunt Patty's road was a narrow two-lane country road with very few houses. The windshield wipers pushed the snow aside, and she sat hunched forward, peering out into the path of the headlights, not daring to glance at the gas gauge.

In the darkness, nothing looked familiar. She rarely came out here, and when she did, Walter always drove. She should have stayed and waited for Aunt Patty, but it was too late now to try to turn around and get back.

"Why are you stopping the car, Mommy?"

Julia put her head down on the wheel. She was not going to panic. She had two children to look after. She had to think clearly.

The baby woke up and began to scream.

"The baby woke up, Mommy."

"I know, sweetheart."

"Why'd you stop the car?"

"Don't get upset, Kevin. We've just run out of gas. Everything will be all right. Just don't get upset."

"I'm not upset. The baby's upset. I'm fidgety."

"Well, you can get out of your seat for a while." She reached back and undid his seat belt. He clambered happily into the front seat.

"Oh, tuna fish," he cursed, four-year-old style. "It's stopped snowing."

Julia took Jenny out of the car bed. One thing at a time. First, the baby must be fed. As she nursed the baby, she began to sing to entertain Kevin, who was jealous that his sister could have her supper while he could not.

They were singing about glories streaming from heaven afar when Kevin spotted the light ahead. "Look, Mommy!"

Jacob had first seen the headlights come quickly over a rise far down the road and then as quickly disappear. He kept walking, swinging his huge flashlight as he went, expecting them to reappear at any moment. Not that it mattered. The car was heading the wrong way for him anyhow, even if by some miracle it was someone who would consider giving him a ride. At least it had stopped snowing. Just then the beam of his flashlight caught a car sitting in the darkness. There were people inside. He hesitated a moment. What if it were a trick? For himself he didn't mind dying. Lord knew he was ready to go, but Arlene needed him now. He had to get to Washington. Yet here, perhaps, was somebody else in need. He started across the road, heading for the driver's side of the car.

Look, Mommy!" Kevin said again. "Glory streams from heaven afar." A strong bright light moved over the rise and down the hill toward them. Julia stopped singing and watched it come. Finally, behind the light, she could make out the tall bulging shadow of a man. She checked quickly to make sure all the doors were locked, took the baby off her breast, and straightened her clothes with a shaking hand. The light was coming straight for her window. Her eyes blinked to shut out the brightness, and when she opened them, a huge black face, which seemed to fill the side window of the small car, was there within inches of her cheek. She pulled back. The man tapped on the window with a worn brown glove that showed the tips of his fingers, and said something through the glass. Julia squeezed the baby tighter and stared straight ahead.

Kevin leaned across her and banged the glass. "Hi!" he said.

"Hi yourself."

Out of the corner of her eye Julia could see the black face smiling broadly. The chin was covered with silver bristles and several teeth were missing. She tried to grab at Kevin to shush him.

"Need some help?" This time the man was shouting as though to make sure she could hear him plainly through the window, but she refused to turn her head.

"Mommy, why don't you answer the nice man?"

"Shh, Kevin. We don't know what he wants."

"He wants to know if we need some help."

The man leaned close to the glass and shouted again. "Don't be afraid, little lady."

"You hear that, Mommy?"

"Kevin, please."

"But, Mommy, he said, 'Don't be afraid!' That's what *angels* say."

"Kevin, no!"

But before she could catch him, Kevin had slid across the seat, pulled up the button, opened the door, and jumped out of the car. The man immediately started around to meet him.

"Don't you touch my child!" Julia screamed, twisting awkwardly from under the wheel, still clutching the baby.

"You don't want him running out into the road, do you, lady?"

"No. No. Thank you." She took Kevin's hand.

"I saw your car and figured you was in trouble."

There was no way to ignore him now. But she had to be careful. He was over six feet tall and obviously strong. The police-pamphlet directions flashed across her brain: *Be sure to look carefully at your assailant so you can give an accurate description to the police later.* If there was a later. Oh, God, don't let him hurt me. Don't let him hurt the children.

"We run out of gas," said Kevin.

Why was she so afraid of him? He, Jacob, who had never willfully hurt the least one of God's creatures—couldn't she tell by looking at him that he only wanted to help? Even the child could see that. He stretched out his hand to put it on the boy's head, but seeing the look in the woman's eyes, he brought it back.

"Your old car's got a empty belly, huh?"

The boy giggled. "Me, too," he said. "I haven't even had my supper."

"Well, we gotta do something about that. I passed a gas station a while back," Jacob said to the woman. "You don't have a can, do you?"

She shook her head. She seemed to be shivering.

"You better get back in the car and try to stay warm." He turned and started back up the hill, sighing as he retraced the descent of a few minutes before. It seemed to have grown steeper. But, at least, praise the Lord, the snow had stopped and the sky was clearing.

"Wait," she called after him. "You'll need some money."

"I got some," Jacob said. He didn't want to waste time and energy going back down the hill.

Suppose he never came back? Would they grow cold and sleepy and freeze out here in the middle of nowhere on Christmas Eve? Well, Aunt Patty, you will have certainly beaten your own record this year—even Christmas morning in the emergency room will pale in comparison. And then suppose he did come back? What did he want? He could have just taken her purse and run, if money was what he wanted. But of course it was the car he was after, so he could get away faster—but she tried not to think of that.

"I think we should sing some more songs," Kevin said. "I might forget about my tummy."

Julia was glad for the diversion. They sang through every carol she knew, even la-la-ing through unfamiliar verses. Then they sang all the songs on Kevin's favorite records, then another round of Christmas carols. Until at long last they saw the light coming over the hill.

"Here comes the glory light," said Kevin.

This time when the man came to her window, she rolled it down. "Would you hold the flashlight for me while I pour the gas in?" he asked.

Trembling, she laid Jenny down in the car bed and went around to the tank. He handed her his big torch, which she tried to hold steady as he poured.

"Well, thank you," Julia said when he had finished, keeping her voice cool. "Let me pay you something for all your trouble."

Jacob looked at her. She was going to give him some money and drive off. He had given her nearly an hour of his time and far more of his energy than he could spare. There was no way she could pay him for that. But she had already gone to the front seat and gotten her purse, the little boy scampering around her at every step.

"That's all right," he said. "Forget it."

She stuck a few bills out at him. "But I owe you for the gas."

"I—uh—do need to return the can. If you could give me a ride down the road and back. . . ."

She nodded.

He could tell by her eyes that she didn't want him in her car, but, Lord, she owed him that much. He decided to ignore her eyes.

"Well, old man," he said to the child, "let's see if we can get this old buggy going." He took the boy around and put him in his seat, letting the child tell him how to buckle the belt, and then climbed into the front seat.

The woman put her purse down between them and buckled herself in. Jacob looked down at her purse and then realized she had caught him looking. He quickly shifted his gaze. "Just down the road a couple miles or so," he said.

Within ten minutes they were at the lighted station. She gave the can back to the attendant and asked him to fill the tank. She saw his eyes question the presence of the man on the seat beside her. Should she try to signal for help? It seemed too foolish. The man had done nothing except try to help her—so far. She at least owed him a ride home on this freezing night.

"We come to get my Aunt Patty to take her home for Christmas." Oh, Kevin.

"Is that a fact? Where's your home, old man?"

Don't answer him, Kevin. But of course Kevin, who had memorized his full address at nursery school, recited it in a proud singsong: "Thirteen-oh-six Essex Street Northwest, Washington, D.C. Two-oh-oh-one-six."

"My, you're one smart boy."

"I know," said Kevin.

I could get a ride all the way to Washington tonight, Jacob said to himself. All I have to do is ask. But he couldn't make himself say the words. If the woman had seemed in the least bit friendly, the least bit trusting, he would have asked her. But how could he ask a favor of a person who thought he was going to grab her purse or hurt her kids?

She had started the car and was pulling out of the station. "Where shall I let you off?" she asked.

It was his chance to tell her. She owed him something, didn't she? And Arlene was waiting, not even knowing if he had gotten her letter.

"Just down the road," he mumbled. "Just anywhere."

They drove past the place where they had met, but he gave no sign of wanting to be let out, so Julia drove on. She couldn't just stop in the middle of nowhere and order him out. What should she do? They went on until she could see Aunt Patty's house ablaze with light. Aunt Patty was home. Thank God for small blessings.

"Here's where Aunt Patty lives," Kevin told the stranger.

"Is that a fact?"

The problem of how to get Aunt Patty without leaving the children alone in the car with the man solved itself. Aunt Patty came rushing out of the house, coat and suitcase flying. She had obviously been watching for the car. When she saw Julia at the wheel, she was furious. "Where have you been?" she demanded. "You're going to make me miss the music."

Julia opened her mouth to defend herself, but at the same moment her passenger got out of the car. He stood there tall and straight against the starry winter sky.

"Mercy!" Aunt Patty screamed. "What in the world?"

"He's our angel, Aunt Patty. Our Christmas angel."

"Don't be ridiculous, Kevin."

Ridiculous indeed! All Julia's fears evaporated in a puff of anger. How dare Aunt Patty call it ridiculous? The man had been an angel. She leaned across the seat and called out, "Would you mind squeezing in back with the children?"

Even in the darkness she thought she could see him smile.

"Get in, Aunt Patty," she commanded, "or you'll make us miss the music."

A little farther down the road she turned to him. "How far can I take you?"

"I need to go all the way to Washington," he said.

"Oh, goody!" cried Kevin. "Then you can go to church with us! We never had a real angel in our church before."

He patted the boy's knee. "Can't make it this time, old man," he said. "I got to go see this lonesome little girl. Cheer her up for Christmas."

"Angels are really busy, aren't they?"

Jacob laughed, a great rich sound which filled the car. "Yeah," he said. "We keep busy, but it's mighty pleasant work."

Aunt Patty may have said something that sounded like "ridiculous," but Julia joyfully chose to ignore it. This was going to be a perfect Christmas.

THE FIR TREE

HANS CHRISTIAN ANDERSEN
(1805–1875)

Far down in the forest, where the warm sun and the fresh air made a sweet resting place, grew a pretty little fir tree. And yet it was not so happy—it wished so much to be tall like its companions, the pines and firs which grew around it. The sun shone, the soft air fluttered its leaves, and the little peasant children passed by, prattling merrily, but the fir tree heeded them not. Sometimes the children would bring a large basket of raspberries or strawberries, wreathed on a straw, and sat themselves near the fir tree and say, "Is this not a pretty little tree?" which made it feel more unhappy than before.

And yet all this while the tree grew a notch or joint taller every year—for by the number of joints in the stem of a fir tree we can discover its age. Still, as it grew it complained, "Oh, how I wish I were as tall as the other trees. Then I would spread out my branches on every side, and my top would overlook the wide world. I should have the birds building their nests on my boughs, and when the wind blew, I should bow with stately dignity like my tall companions."

The tree was so discontented that it took no pleasure in the warm sunshine, the birds, or the rosy clouds that floated over it morning and evening. Sometimes in winter, when the snow lay white and glittering on the ground, a hare would come springing along and would jump right over the little tree, and then how mortified it would feel!

Two winters passed; and when the third arrived, the tree had grown so tall that the hare was obliged to run round it. Yet it remained dissatisfied and would exclaim, "Oh, if I could but keep on growing tall and old! There is nothing else worth caring for in the world."

In the autumn, as usual, the woodcutters came and cut down several of the tallest trees. And the young fir tree, which was not grown to its full height, shuddered as the noble trees fell to the earth with a crash. After the branches were lopped off, the trunks looked so slender and bare that they could scarcely be recognized. Then they were placed upon wagons and drawn by horses out of the forest. Where were they going? What would become of them? The young fir tree wished very much to know. So in the spring, when the swallows and the storks came, it asked, "Do you know where those trees were taken? Did you meet them?"

The swallows knew nothing, but the stork, after a little reflection, nodded his head and said, "Yes, I think I do. I met several new ships when I flew from Egypt, and they had masts that smelt like fir. I think these must have been the trees. I assure you they were stately, very stately."

"Oh, how I wish I were tall enough to go on the sea," said the fir tree. "What is this sea, and what is it like?"

"It would take too much time to explain," said the stork, flying quickly away.

"Rejoice in thy youth," said the sunbeam. "Rejoice in thy fresh growth and the young life that is in thee." And the wind kissed the tree and the dew watered it with tears, but the fir tree regarded them not.

Christmas drew near and many young trees were cut down, some even smaller and younger than the fir tree, who enjoyed neither rest nor peace from longing to leave its forest home. These young trees, chosen for their beauty, kept their branches, but they too were laid on wagons and drawn by horses out of the forest.

"Where are they going?" asked the fir tree. "They are no taller than I am. Indeed, one is much shorter. And why are the branches not cut off? Where are they going?"

"We know. We know," sang the sparrows. "We have looked in at the windows of the houses in town, and we know what is done with them. They are dressed up in the most splendid manner. We have seen them standing in the middle of a warm room, and adorned with all sorts of beautiful things—honey cakes, gilded apples, playthings, and many hundreds of wax tapers."

"And then," asked the fir tree, trembling through all its branches, "and then what happens?"

"We did not see any more," said the sparrows. "But that was enough for us."

"I wonder whether anything so brilliant will ever happen to me," thought the fir tree. "It would be much better than crossing the sea. I long for it almost with pain. Oh, when will Christmas be here? I am now as tall and well grown as those which were taken away last year. Oh, that I were now laid on the wagon, or standing in the warm room, with all that brightness and splendor around me! Something better and more beautiful is to come after, or the trees would not be so decked out. What can it be? I am weary with longing. I scarcely know how I feel."

"Rejoice with us," said the air and the sunlight. "Enjoy thine own bright life in the fresh air."

But the tree would not rejoice, though it grew taller every day. And in winter and summer its dark green foliage might be seen in the forest, while passers-by would say, "What a beautiful tree!"

A short time before Christmas, the discontented fir tree was the first to fall. As the ax cut through the stem and divided the pith, the tree fell with a groan to the earth, conscious of pain and faintness, and forgetting all its anticipations of happiness in sorrow at leaving its home in the forest. It knew that it should never again see its dear old companions, the trees, nor the little bushes and many-colored flowers that had grown by its side; perhaps not even the birds. Neither was the journey at all pleasant. The tree first recovered itself while being unpacked with several other trees in the courtyard of a house, and it heard a man say, "We want only one, and this is the prettiest."

Then came two servants in grand livery and carried the fir tree into a large and beautiful apartment. On the walls hung pictures and near the great stove stood great china vases, with lions on the lids. There were rocking chairs, silken sofas, and large tables covered with pictures, books, and playthings worth a great deal of money. At least, the children said so. Then the fir tree was placed in a large tub full of sand, but green baize hung all around it so that no one could see it was a tub, and it stood on a very handsome carpet.

How the fir tree trembled! "What is going to happen to me now?" Some young ladies came and the servants helped them to adorn the tree. On one branch they hung little bags cut out of colored paper, and each bag was filled with sweetmeats. From other branches hung gilded apples and walnuts as if they had grown there. And above and all around were hundreds of red, blue, and white tapers, which were fastened on the branches. Dolls exactly like real babies were placed under the green leaves—the tree had never seen such things before! And at the very top was fastened a glittering star made of tinsel. Oh, it was very beautiful!

"This evening," they all exclaimed, "how bright it will be!"

"Oh, that the evening were here!" thought the tree. "And the tapers lighted! Then I shall know what else is going to happen. Will the trees of the forest come to see me? I wonder if the sparrows will peep in at the windows as they fly? Shall I grow faster here, and keep on all these ornaments during summer and winter?" But guessing was of very little use. It made his bark ache, and this pain is as bad for a slender fir tree as a headache is for us. At last the tapers were lighted and then what a glistening blaze of light the tree presented! It trembled so with joy in all its branches that one of the candles fell among the green leaves and burnt some of them. "Help! Help!" exclaimed the young ladies, but there was no danger, for they quickly extinguished the fire. After this the tree tried not to tremble at all, though the fire frightened him. He was so anxious not to hurt any of the beautiful ornaments, even while their brilliancy dazzled him.

And now the folding doors were thrown open and a troop of children rushed in as if they intended to upset the tree. They were followed more slowly by their elders. For a moment the little ones stood silent with astonishment, and then they shouted for joy till the room rang, and they danced merrily round the tree, while one present after another was taken from it.

"What are they doing? What will happen next?" thought the fir. At last the candles burnt down to the branches and were put out. Then the children received permission to plunder the tree.

Oh, how they rushed upon it, till the branches cracked, and had it not been fastened with the glistening star to the ceiling, it might have been thrown down. The children then danced about with their pretty toys, and no one noticed the tree except the children's maid, who came and peeped among the branches to see if an apple or a fig had been forgotten. "A story! A story!" cried the children, pulling a little fat man towards the tree.

"Now we shall be in the green shade," said the man, as he seated himself under it, "and the tree will have the pleasure of hearing also, but I shall only relate one story. What shall it be?

Ivede-Avede? Or Humpty Dumpty, who fell downstairs but soon got up again, and at last married a princess?"

"Ivede-Avede," cried some. "Humpty Dumpty," cried others, and there was a fine shouting and crying out. The fir tree remained quite still and thought to himself, "Shall I have anything to do with all this?" But he had already amused them as much as they wished. Then the old man told them the story of Humpty Dumpty—how he fell downstairs, and was raised up again, and married a princess. And the children clapped their hands and cried, "Tell another! Tell another!" They wanted to hear the story of Ivede-Avede, but they only had Humpty Dumpty. After this the fir tree became quite silent and thoughtful. Never had the birds in the forest told such tales as Humpty Dumpty, who fell downstairs and yet married a princess.

"Ah, yes, so it happens in the world," thought the fir tree. He believed it all, because it was related by such a nice man. "Ah, well," he thought, "who knows? Perhaps I may fall down too, and marry a princess." And he looked forward joyfully to the next evening, expecting to be again decked out with lights and playthings, gold and fruit. "Tomorrow I will not tremble," thought he. "I will enjoy all my splendor, and I shall hear the story of Humpty Dumpty again, and perhaps Ivede-Avede." And the tree remained quiet and thoughtful all night. In the morning the servants and the housemaid came in.

"Now," thought the fir, "all my splendor is going to begin again." But they dragged him out of the room and upstairs to the garret and threw him on the floor, in a dark corner where no daylight shone, and there they left him.

"What does this mean?" thought the tree. "What am I to do here? I can hear nothing in a place like this!" And he leaned against the wall and thought and thought.

He had time enough to think, for days and nights passed and no one came near him, and when at last somebody did come, it was only to put away large boxes in a corner. So the tree was completely hidden from sight as if it had never existed. "It is winter now," thought the tree. "The ground is hard and covered with snow, so that people cannot plant me. I shall be sheltered here, I daresay, until spring comes. How thoughtful and kind everybody is to me! Still I wish this place were not so dark as well as lonely, with not even a little hare to look at. How pleasant it was out in the forest when the snow lay on the ground. Then the hare would run by, yes, and jump over me too, although I did not like it then. Oh, it is terribly lonely here!"

"Squeak, squeak," said a little mouse, creeping cautiously towards the tree. Then came another, and they both sniffed at the fir tree and crept between the branches.

"Oh, it is very cold," said the mouse, "or else we should be so comfortable here, shouldn't we, you old fir tree?"

"I am not old," said the fir tree. "There are many who are older than I am."

"Where do you come from and what do you know?" asked the mice, who were full of curiosity. "Have you seen the most beautiful places in the world, and can you tell us all about them? And have you been in the storeroom, where cheeses lie on the shelf and hams hang from the ceiling? One can run about on tallow candles there, and go in thin and come out fat."

"I know nothing of that place," said the fir tree. "But I know the wood where the sun shines and the birds sing."

And then the tree told the little mice all about its youth. They had never heard such an account in their lives. After they had listened to it attentively, they said, "What a number of things you have seen! You must have been very happy."

"Happy?" exclaimed the fir tree. And then as he reflected upon what he had been telling them, he said, "Ah, yes. After all, those were happy days." But when he went on and related all about

Christmas Eve, and how he had been dressed up with cakes and lights, the mice said, "How happy you must have been, you old fir tree!"

"I am not old at all," replied the tree. "I only came from the forest this winter. I am now checked in my growth."

"What splendid stories you can relate," said the little mice. And the next night four other mice came with them to hear what the tree had to tell. The more he talked, the more he remembered, and then he thought to himself, "Those were happy days, but they may come again. Humpty Dumpty fell downstairs, and yet he married the princess. Perhaps I may marry a princess too." And the fir tree thought of the pretty little birch tree that grew in the forest, which was to him a real, beautiful princess.

"Who is Humpty Dumpty?" asked the little mice, and then the tree related the whole story. He could remember every single word, and the little mice were so delighted with it that they were ready to jump to the top of the tree. The next night a great many more mice came, and on Sunday two rats came with them. But the rats said it was not a pretty story at all, and the little mice were very sorry, for it made them also think less of it.

"Do you know only one story?" asked the rats.

"Only one," replied the fir tree. "I heard it on the happiest evening in my life, but I did not know I was so happy at the time."

"We think it is a very miserable story," said the rats. "Don't you know any story about bacon or tallow in the storeroom?"

"No," replied the tree.

"Many thanks to you then," replied the rats, and they marched off.

The little mice also kept away after this, and the tree sighed and said, "It was very pleasant when the merry little mice sat round me and listened while I talked. Now that is all past too. However, I shall consider myself happy when someone comes to take me out of this place." But would this ever happen? Yes, one morning people came to clear out the garret. The boxes were packed away, and the tree was pulled out of the corner and thrown roughly on the garret floor. Then the servant dragged it out upon the staircase where the daylight shone.

"Now life is beginning again," said the tree, rejoicing in the sunshine and fresh air. Then it was carried downstairs and taken into the courtyard so quickly that it forgot to think of itself, and could only look about. There was so much to be seen! The court was close to a garden, where everything looked blooming. Fresh and fragrant roses hung over the little palings. The linden trees were in blossom, while the swallows flew here and there, crying, "Twit, twit, twit, my mate is coming." But it was not the fir tree they meant.

"Now I shall live," cried the tree, joyfully spreading out its branches. But alas, they were all withered and yellow, and it lay in a corner amongst weeds and nettles. The star of gold paper was still stuck in the top of the tree and glittered in the sunshine. In the same courtyard were playing two of the merry children who had danced round the tree at Christmas and had been so happy. The youngest saw the gilded star and ran and pulled it off the tree.

"Look what is sticking to the old ugly fir tree," said the child, treading on the branches till they crackled under his boots. And the tree saw all the fresh bright flowers in the garden, and then looked at itself and wished it had remained in the dark corner of the garret. It thought of its fresh youth in the forest, of the merry Christmas evening, and of the little mice who had listened to the story of Humpty Dumpty.

"Past! past!" said the old tree. "Oh, had I but enjoyed myself while I could have done so! Now it is too late."

Then a lad came and chopped the tree into small pieces, till a large bundle lay in a heap on the ground. The pieces were placed in a fire under the kettle, and they quickly blazed up brightly, while the tree sighed so deeply that each sigh was like a little pistol shot. Then the children, who were at play, came and seated themselves in front of the fire, and looked at it and cried, "Pop, pop." But at each "pop," which was a deep sigh, the tree was thinking of a summer day in the forest, or of some winter night there when the stars shone brightly, and of Christmas evening, and of Humpty Dumpty, the only story it had ever heard or knew how to relate—till at last it was consumed.

The boys still played in the garden, and the youngest wore on his breast the golden star with which the tree had been adorned during the happiest evening of its existence. Now all was past: the tree's life was past, and the story also—for all stories must come to an end at last.

CHILD

ELIZABETH ROONEY
(1924–)

Dear child, sweet child,
Sleeping in the straw,
We who come to worship you
Kneel now in awe.

Dear child, sweet child,
Sheltered in a stable,
Each of us would bring you
Gifts, as we are able.

Dear child, sweet child,
Lighted by a star,
Help our hearts to find you
No matter where we are.

Dear child, sweet child,
Willing to be man,
Teach us how to love you.
No one else can.

WHERE LOVE IS, THERE GOD IS ALSO

LEO TOLSTOY
(1828–1910)

In a certain city dwelt Martin Avdyeeich, the cobbler. He lived in a cellar, a wretched little hole with a single window. The window looked up towards the street, and through it Martin could just see the passers-by. It is true that he could see little more than their boots, but Martin Avdyeeich could read a man's character by his boots, so he needed no more. Martin had lived long in that one place, and had many acquaintances. Few indeed were the boots in that neighborhood which had not passed through his hands at some time or other. On some he would fasten new soles, to others he would give side-pieces, others again he would stitch all round, and even give them new uppers if need be. And often he saw his own handiwork through the window. There was always lots of work for him, for Avdyeeich's hand was cunning and his leather good; nor did he overcharge, and he always kept his word. He always engaged to do a job by a fixed time if he could; but if he could not, he said so at once, and deceived no man. So everyone knew Avdyeeich, and he had no lack of work.

Avdyeeich had always been a pretty good man, but as he grew old he began to think more about his soul, and draw nearer to his God. While Martin was still a journeyman his wife had died; but his wife had left him a little boy—three years old. Their other children had not lived. All the eldest had died early. Martin wished at first to send his little child into the country to his sister, but afterwards he thought better of it. "My Kapitoshka," thought he, "will feel miserable in a strange household. He shall stay here with me." And so Avdyeeich left his master, and took to living in lodgings alone with his little son.

But God did not give Avdyeeich happiness in his children. No sooner had the little one begun to grow up and be a help and a joy to his father's heart, than a sickness fell upon Kapitoshka. The little one took to his bed, lay there in a raging fever for a week, and then died. Martin buried his son in despair—so desperate was he that he began to murmur against God. Such disgust of life overcame him that he more than once begged God that he might die; and he reproached God for taking not him, an old man, but his darling, his only son, instead. And after that Avdyeeich left off going to church.

And lo! one day, there came to Avdyeeich from the Troitsa Monastery, an aged peasant-pilgrim—it was already the eighth year of his pilgrimage. Avdyeeich fell a-talking with him and began to complain of his great sorrow. "As for living any longer, thou man of God," said he, "I desire it not. Would only that I might die! That is my sole prayer to God. I am now a man who has no hope."

And the old man said to him: "Thy speech, Martin, is not good. How shall we judge the doings of God? God's judgments are not our thoughts. God willed that thy son shouldst die, but that thou shouldst live. Therefore 'twas the best thing both for him and for thee. It is because thou wouldst fain have lived for thy own delight that thou dost now despair."

"But what then *is* a man to live for?" asked Avdyeeich.

And the old man answered: "For God, Martin! He gave thee life, and for Him therefore must thou live. When thou dost begin to live for Him, thou wilt grieve about nothing more, and all things will come easy to thee."

Martin was silent for a moment, and then he said: "And how must one live for God?"

"Christ hath shown us the way. Thou knowest thy letters. Buy the Gospels and read; there thou wilt find out how to live for God. There everything is explained."

These words made the heart of Avdyeeich burn within him, and he went the same day and bought for himself a New Testament printed in very large type, and began to read.

Avdyeeich set out with the determination to read it only on holidays; but as he read, it did his heart so much good that he took to reading it every day. And the second time he read until all the kerosene in the lamp had burnt itself out, and for all that he could not tear himself away from the book. And so it was every evening. And the more he read, the more clearly he understood what God wanted of him, and how it behooved him to live for God; and his heart grew lighter and lighter continually. Formerly, whenever he lay down to sleep he would only sigh and groan, and think of nothing but Kapitoshka, but now he would only say to himself: "Glory to Thee! Glory to Thee, O Lord! Thy will be done!"

Henceforth the whole life of Avdyeeich was changed. Formerly, whenever he had a holiday, he would go to the tavern to drink tea, nor would he say no to a drop of brandy now and again, and would leave the inn a bit merry, babbling nonsense and talking loudly and censoriously. He was done with all that now. His life became quiet and joyful. With the morning light he sat down to his work, worked out his time, then took down his lamp from the hook, placed it on the table, took down his book from the shelf, bent over it, and sat down to read. And the more he read the more he understood, and his heart grew brighter and happier.

It happened once that Martin was up reading till very late. He was reading St. Luke's Gospel. He was reading the sixth chapter, and as he read he came to the words: "And to him that smiteth thee on the one cheek, offer also the other." This passage he read several times, and presently he came to that place where the Lord says: "And why call ye me Lord, Lord, and do not the things which I say? Whosoever cometh to Me, and heareth My sayings, and doeth them, I will show you to whom he is like. He is like a man which built an house, and dug deep, and laid the foundations on a rock. And when the flood arose, the storm beat vehemently upon that house, and could not shake it, for it was founded upon a rock. But he that heareth, and doeth not, is like a man that without a foundation built an house upon the earth, against which the stream did beat vehemently, and immediately it fell, and the ruin of that house was great."

Avdyeeich read these words through and through, and his heart was glad. He took off his glasses, laid them on the book, rested his elbow on the table, and fell a-thinking. And he began to measure his own life by these words. And he thought to himself, "Is my house built on the rock or on the sand? How good to be as on a rock! How easy it all seems to thee sitting alone here. It seems as if thou wert doing God's will to the full, and so thou takest no heed and fallest away again. And yet thou wouldst go on striving, for so it is good for thee. O Lord, help me!"

Thus thought he, and would have lay down, but it was a grief to tear himself away from the book. And so he began reading the seventh chapter. He read all about the Centurion, he read all about the Widow's Son, he read all about the answer to the disciples of St. John; and so he came to that place where the rich Pharisee invites our Lord to be his guest. And he read all about how the woman who was a sinner anointed His feet and washed them with her tears, and how He justified her. And so he came at last to the forty-fourth verse, and there he read these words, "And He turned to the woman and said to Simon, Seest thou this woman? I entered into thine house, thou gavest Me no water for My feet; but she has washed My feet with tears and wiped them with the hairs of her head. Thou gavest Me no kiss, but this woman, since the time I came in, hath not ceased to kiss My feet. Mine head with oil thou didst not anoint." And again Avdyeeich took off his glasses, and laid them on the book, and fell a-thinking.

"So it is quite plain that I too have something of the Pharisee about me. Am I not always thinking of myself? Am I not always thinking of drinking tea, and keeping myself as warm and cozy as possible, without thinking at all about the guest? Simon thought about himself, but did not give the slightest thought to his guest. But who was the guest? The Lord Himself. And suppose He were to come to me, should I treat Him as the Pharisee did?"

And Avdyeeich leaned both his elbows on the table and, without perceiving it, fell a-dozing.

"Martin!"—it was as though the voice of someone close to his ear.

Martin started up from his nap. "Who's there?"

He turned round, he gazed at the door, but there was no one. Again he dozed off. Suddenly he heard quite plainly, "Martin, Martin, I say! Look tomorrow into the street. I am coming."

Martin awoke, rose from his chair, and began to rub his eyes. And he did not know himself whether he had heard these words asleep or awake. He turned down the lamp and lay down to rest.

At dawn the next day, Avdyeeich arose, prayed to God, lit his stove, got ready his gruel and cabbage soup, filled his samovar, put on his apron, and sat down by his window to work. There Avdyeeich sits and works, and thinks of nothing but the things of yesternight. His thoughts were divided. He thought at one time that he must have gone off dozing, and then again he thought he really must have heard that voice. It might have been so, he thought.

Martin sits at the window and looks as much at his window as at his work, and whenever a strange pair of boots passes by he bends forward and looks out of the window, so as to see the face as well as the feet of the passers-by. The house porter passed by in new felt boots, the water-carrier passed by, and after that there passed close to the window an old soldier, one of Nicholas's veterans, in tattered old boots, with a shovel in his hands. Avdyeeich knew him by his boots. The old fellow was called Stepanuich, and lived with the neighboring shopkeeper, who harbored him of his charity. His duty was to help the porter. Stepanuich stopped before Avdyeeich's window to sweep away the snow. Avdyeeich cast a glance at him, and then went on working as before.

"I'm not growing wiser as I grow older," thought Avdyeeich, with some self-contempt. "I make up my mind that Christ is coming to me, and lo! 'tis only Stepanuich clearing away the snow. Thou simpleton, thou! Thou art wool-gathering!" Then Avdyeeich made ten more stitches, and then he stretched his head once more towards the window. He looked through the window again, and there he saw that Stepanuich had placed the shovel against the wall, and was warming himself and taking breath a bit.

"The old man is very much broken," thought Avdyeeich to himself. "It is quite plain that he has scarcely strength enough to scrape away the snow. Suppose I make him drink a little tea! The samovar, too, is just on the boil." Avdyeeich put down his awl, got up, placed the samovar on the table, put some tea in it, and tapped on the window with his fingers. Stepanuich turned round and came to the window. Avdyeeich beckoned to him, and then went and opened the door.

"Come in and warm yourself a bit," cried he, "You're a bit chilled, eh?"

"Christ requite you! Yes, and all my bones ache too," said Stepanuich. Stepanuich came in, shook off the snow, and began to wipe his feet so as not to soil the floor, but he tottered sadly.

"Don't trouble about wiping your feet. I'll rub it off myself. It's all in the day's work. Come in and sit down," said Avdyeeich. "Here, take a cup of tea."

And Avdyeeich filled two cups, and gave one to his guest, and he poured his own tea out into the saucer and began to blow it.

Stepanuich drank his cup, turned it upside down, put a gnawed crust on the top of it, and said, "Thank you." But it was quite plain that he wanted to be asked to have some more.

"Have a drop more. Do!" said Avdyeeich, and poured out fresh cups for his guest and himself, and as Avdyeeich drank his cup, he could not help glancing at the window from time to time.

"Dost thou expect any one?" asked his guest.

"Do I expect any one? Well, honestly, I hardly know. I am expecting and I am not expecting, and there's a word which has burnt itself right into my heart. Whether it was a vision or no, I know not. Look now, my brother! I was reading yesterday about our little Father Christ, how He suffered, how He came on earth. Hast thou heard of Him, eh?"

"I have heard, I have heard," replied Stepanuich, "but we poor ignorant ones know not our letters."

"Anyhow, I was reading about this very thing—how He came down upon earth. I was reading how He went to the Pharisee, and how the Pharisee did not meet Him halfway. That was what I was reading about yesternight, little brother mine. I read that very thing, and bethought me how the Honorable did not receive our little Father Christ honorably. But suppose, I thought, if He came to one like me—would I receive Him? Simon at any rate did not receive Him at all. Thus I thought, and so thinking, fell asleep. I fell asleep, I say, little brother mine, and I heard my name called. I started up. A voice was whispering at my very ear. 'Look out to-morrow!' it said. 'I am coming.' And so it befell twice. Now look! wouldst thou believe it? The idea stuck to me—I scold myself for my folly, and yet I look for Him, our little Father Christ!"

Stepanuich shook his head and said nothing, but he drank his cup dry and put it aside. Then Avdyeeich took up the cup and filled it again.

"Drink some more. 'Twill do thee good. Now it seems to me that when our little Father went about on earth, He despised no one, but sought unto the simple folk most of all. He was always among the simple folk. Those disciples of His too, He chose most of them from amongst our brother-laborers, sinners like us. He that exalteth himself, He says, shall be abased, and he that abaseth himself shall be exalted. Ye, says He, call me Lord, and I, says He, wash your feet. He who would be the first among you, He says, let him become the servant of all. And therefore it is that He says, Blessed are the lowly, the peacemakers, the humble, and the long-suffering."

Stepanuich forgot his tea. He was an old man, softhearted, and tearful. He sat and listened, and the tears rolled down his cheeks.

"Come, drink a little more," said Avdyeeich. But Stepanuich crossed himself, expressed his thanks, pushed away his cup, and got up.

"I thank thee, Martin Avdyeeich. I have fared well at thy hands, and thou hast refreshed me both in body and soul."

"Thou wilt show me a kindness by coming again. I am so glad to have a guest," said Avdyeeich. Stepanuich departed, and Martin poured out the last drop of tea, drank it, washed up, and again sat down by the window to work—he had some back-stitching to do. He stitched and stitched, and now and then cast glances at the window—he was looking for Christ, and could think of nothing but Him and His works. And the many sayings of Christ were in his head all the time.

Two soldiers passed by, one in regimental boots, the other in boots of his own making. After that, the owner of the next house passed by in nicely brushed galoshes. A baker with a basket also passed by. All these passed by in turn, and then there came alongside the window a woman in worsted stockings and rustic shoes, and as she was passing by she stopped short in front of the partition wall. Avdyeeich looked up at her from his window, and he saw that the woman was a stranger and poorly clad, and that she had a little child with her. She was leaning up against the wall with her back to the wind, and tried to wrap the child up, but she had nothing to wrap it up with. The woman wore summer clothes, and thin enough they were. And from out of his corner Avdyeeich heard the child crying and the woman trying to comfort it, but she could not. Then Avdyeeich got up, went out of the door and on to the steps, and cried, "My good woman! My good woman!"

The woman heard him and turned round.

"Why dost thou stand out in the cold there with the child? Come inside! In the warm room thou wilt be better able to tend him. This way!"

The woman was amazed. What she saw was an old fellow in an apron and with glasses on his nose calling to her. She came towards him.

They went down the steps together and into the room. The old man led the woman to the bed. "There," said he, "sit down nearer to the stove, and warm and feed thy little one."

He went to the table, got some bread and a dish, opened the oven door, put some cabbage soup into the dish, took out a pot of gruel, but it was not quite ready, so he put some cabbage soup only into the dish, and placed it on the table. Then he fetched bread, took down the cloth from the hook, and spread it on the table.

"Sit down and have something to eat, dear lady," said he, "and I will sit down a little with the youngster. I have had children of my own, and know how to manage them."

The woman crossed herself, sat down at the table, and began to eat, and Avdyeeich sat down on the bed with the child. Avdyeeich smacked his lips at him again and again, but his lack of teeth made it a clumsy joke at best. And all the time the child never left off shrieking. Then Avdyeeich hit upon the idea of shaking his finger at him, so he snapped his fingers up and down, backwards and forwards, right in front of the child's mouth. He did not put his finger into its mouth, because his finger was black and sticky with cobbler's wax. And the child stared at the finger and was silent, and presently it began to laugh. And Avdyeeich was delighted. But the woman went on eating, and told him who she was and whence she came.

"I am a soldier's wife," she said. "My eight months' husband they drove right away from me, and nothing has been heard of him since. I took a cook's place till I became a mother. They could not keep me *and* the child. It is now three months since I have been drifting about without any fixed resting-place. I have eaten away my all. I wanted to be a wet-nurse, but people wouldn't have me: 'Thou art too thin,' they said. I have just been to the merchant's wife where our grandmother lives, and there they promised to take me in. I thought it was all right, but she told me to come again in a week. But she lives a long way off. I am chilled to death, and he is quite tired out. But God be praised! Our landlady has compassion on us, and gives us shelter for Christ's sake. But for that I don't know how we could live through it all."

Avdyeeich sighed, and said, "And have you no warm clothes?"

"Ah, kind friend! this is indeed warm-clothes time, but yesterday I pawned away my last shawl for two *grivenki.*"

The woman went to the bed and took up the child, but Avdyeeich stood up, went to the wall cupboard, rummaged about a bit, and then brought back with him an old jacket.

"Look!" said he, " 'tis a shabby thing, but it will do to wrap up in."

The woman looked at the old jacket, then she gazed at the old man, and, taking the jacket, fell a-weeping. Avdyeeich also turned away, crept under the bed, drew out a trunk and seemed to be very busy about it, whereupon he again sat down opposite the woman.

Then the woman said: "Christ requite thee, dear little father! It is plain that it was He who sent me by thy window. When I first came out it was warm, and now it has turned very cold. And He it was, little father, who made thee look out of the window and have compassion on wretched me."

Avdyeeich smiled slightly, and said: "Yes, He must have done it, for I looked not out of the window in vain, dear woman!"

And Avdyeeich told his dream to the soldier's wife also, and how he had heard a voice promising that the Lord should come to him that day.

"All things are possible," said the woman. Then she rose up, put on the jacket, wrapped it round her little one, and then began to curtsey and thank Avdyeeich once more.

"Take this for Christ's sake," said Avdyeeich, giving her a two-grivenka piece, "and redeem your shawl." The woman crossed herself, Avdyeeich crossed himself, and then he led the woman to the door.

The woman went away. Avdyeeich ate up the remainder of the cabbage soup, washed up, and again sat down to work. He worked on and on, but he did not forget the window, and whenever the window was darkened he immediately looked up to see who was passing. Acquaintances passed, strangers passed, but there was no one in particular.

But now Avdyeeich sees how, right in front of his window, an old woman, a huckster, has taken her stand. She carries a basket of apples. Not many now remained; she had evidently sold them nearly all. Across her shoulder she carried a sack full of shavings. She must have picked them up near some new building, and was taking them home with her. It was plain that the sack was straining her shoulder. She wanted to shift it on to the other shoulder, so she rested the sack on the pavement, placed the apple-basket on a small post, and set about shaking down the shavings in the sack. Now while she was shaking down the sack, an urchin in a ragged cap suddenly turned up, goodness knows from whence, grabbed at one of the apples in the basket, and would have made off with it, but the wary old woman turned quickly round and gripped the youth by the sleeve. The lad fought and tried to tear himself loose, but the old woman seized him with both hands, knocked his hat off, and tugged hard at his hair. The lad howled, and the old woman reviled him. Avdyeeich did not stop to put away his awl, but pitched it on the floor, rushed into the courtyard, and in his haste stumbled on the steps and dropped his glasses. Avdyeeich ran out into the street. The old woman was tugging at the lad's hair and wanted to drag him off to the police, while the boy fought and kicked.

"I didn't take it," said he. "What are you whacking me for? Let me go!"

Avdyeeich came up and tried to part them. He seized the lad by the arm and said: "Let him go, little mother! Forgive him for Christ's sake!"

"I'll forgive him so that he shan't forget the taste of fresh birch-rods. I mean to take the rascal to the police station."

Avdyeeich began to entreat with the old woman.

"Let him go, little mother; he will not do so any more. Let him go for Christ's sake."

The old woman let him go. The lad would have bolted, but Avdyeeich held him fast.

"Beg the little mother's pardon," said he, "and don't do such things any more. I saw thee take it."

Then the lad began to cry and beg pardon.

"Well, that's all right! And now, there's an apple for thee." And Avdyeeich took one out of the basket and gave it to the boy. "I'll pay thee for it, little mother," he said to the old woman.

"Thou wilt ruin them that way," said the old woman. "If I had the rewarding of him, he should not be able to sit down for a week."

"Oh, little mother, little mother!" cried Avdyeeich, "that is our way of looking at things, but it is not God's way. If we ought to be whipped so for the sake of one apple, what do we deserve for our sins?"

The old woman was silent.

And Avdyeeich told the old woman about the parable of the master who forgave his servant a very great debt, and how that servant immediately went out and caught his fellow-servant by the throat because he was his debtor. The old woman listened to the end, and the lad listened too.

"God bade us forgive," said Avdyeeich, "otherwise He will not forgive us. We must forgive everyone, especially the thoughtless."

The old woman shook her head and sighed.

"That's all very well," she said, "but they are spoiled enough already."

"Then it is for us old people to teach them better," said Avdyeeich.

"So say I," replied the old woman. "I had seven of them at one time, and now I have but a single daughter left." And the old woman began telling him where and how she lived with her daughter, and how many grandchildren she had. "I'm not what I was," she said, "but I work all I can. I am sorry for my grandchildren, and good children they are, too. No one is so glad to see me as they are. Little Aksyutka will go to none but me. 'Grandma dear! darling grandma!'" and the old woman was melted to tears. "As for him," she added, pointing to the lad, "boys will be boys, I suppose. Well, God be with him!"

Now just as the old woman was about to hoist the sack on to her shoulder, the lad rushed forward and said:

"Give it here, and I'll carry it for thee, granny! It is all in my way."

The old woman shook her head, but she did put the sack on the lad's shoulder.

And so they trudged down the street together side by side. And the old woman forgot to ask Avdyeeich for the money for the apple. Avdyeeich kept standing and looking after them, and heard how they talked to each other, as they went, about all sorts of things.

Avdyeeich followed them with his eyes till they were out of sight, then he turned homewards and found his glasses on the steps (they were not broken), picked up his awl, and sat down to work again. He worked away for a little while, but soon he was scarcely able to distinguish the stitches, and he saw the lamplighter going round to light the lamps. "I see it is time to light up," thought he, so he trimmed his little lamp, lighted it, and again sat down to work. He finished one boot completely, turned it round and inspected it. "Good!" he cried. He put away his tools, swept up the cuttings, removed the brushes and tips, put away the awl, took down the lamp, placed it on the table, and took down the Gospels from the shelf. He wanted to find the passage where he had last evening placed a strip of morocco leather by way of a marker, but he lit upon another place. And just as Avdyeeich opened the Gospel, he recollected his dream of yesterday evening. And no sooner did he call it to mind than it seemed to him as if some persons were moving about and shuffling with their feet behind him. Avdyeeich glanced round and saw that somebody was indeed standing in the dark corner—yes, someone was really there, but who, he could not exactly make out. Then a voice whispered in his ear:

"Martin! Martin! dost thou not know me?"

"Who art thou?" cried Avdyeeich.

" 'Tis I," cried the voice, "lo, 'tis I!" And from the dark corner stepped Stepanuich. He smiled, and it was as though a little cloud were breaking, and he was gone.

"It is I!" cried the voice, and from the corner stepped a woman with a little child; and the woman smiled and the child laughed, and they also disappeared.

"And it is I!" cried the voice, and the old woman and the lad with the apple stepped forth, and both of them smiled, and they also disappeared.

And the heart of Avdyeeich was glad. He crossed himself, put on his glasses, and began to read the Gospels at the place where he had opened them. And at the top of the page he read these words: "And I was an hungered and thirsty, and ye gave Me to drink. I was a stranger and ye took Me in."

And at the bottom of the page he read this: "Inasmuch as ye have done it to the least of these My brethren, ye have done it unto Me."

And Avdyeeich understood that his dream had not deceived him, and that the Savior had really come to him that day, and he had really received Him.

WONDER

This is the irrational season
When love blooms bright and wild.
Had Mary been filled with reason
There'd have been no room for the child.

MADELEINE L'ENGLE

YES, VIRGINIA, THERE IS A SANTA CLAUS

FRANCIS P. CHURCH
(1839–1906)

Francis Church was an editorial writer for the New York Sun. *In September of 1897 he received the following letter from a little girl. His reply to her query has become a classic statement of the true spirit of Christmas.*

Dear Editor:
I am 8 years old. Some of my little friends say there is no Santa Claus. Papa says "If you see it in The Sun, *it's so." Please tell me the truth, is there a Santa Claus?*

Virginia O'Hanlon
115 West 95th Street
New York City

Yes, Virginia, there is a Santa Claus. He exists as certainly as love and generosity and devotion exist, and you know that they abound and give to your life its highest beauty and joy. Alas! how dreary would be the world if there were no Santa Claus! It would be as dreary as if there were no Virginias.

There would be no childlike faith then, no poetry, no romance to make tolerable this existence. We should have no enjoyment, except in sense and sight. The eternal light with which childhood fills the world would be extinguished. Not believe in Santa Claus! You might as well not believe in fairies! You might get your papa to hire men to watch in all the chimneys on Christmas Eve to catch Santa Claus, but even if they did not see Santa Claus coming down, what would that prove? Nobody sees Santa Claus, but that is no sign that there is no Santa Claus. The most real things in the world are those that no children or men can see. Did you ever see fairies dancing on the lawn? Of course not, but that's no proof that they are not there. Nobody can conceive or imagine all the wonders there are unseen or unseeable in the world. . . . No Santa Claus! Thank God he lives, and he lives forever. A thousand years from now, Virginia, nay, ten times ten thousand years from now, he will continue to make glad the heart of childhood.

WINTER

JAMES HURNARD
(1808–1881)

Then comes the Winter, like a hale old man
Wrapped in his cloak with frosty locks and beard.
Winter is the time for clear cold starlight nights,
And driving snows, and frozen roads and rivers,
For crowding round the blazing Christmas fire,
For telling tales that make the blood run cold,
For sipping elder-wine and cracking filberts,
For friendships, chilblains, fun, roast beef, mince pies,
And shivering fits on jumping into bed:
And thus the year goes round, and round, and round.

Snow-Bound

JOHN GREENLEAF WHITTIER
(1807–1892)

The sun that brief December day
Rose cheerless over hills of gray,
And, darkly circled, gave at noon
A sadder light than waning moon.
Slow tracing down the thickening sky
Its mute and ominous prophecy,
A portent seeming less than threat,
It sank from sight before it set.
A chill no coat, however stout,
Of homespun stuff could quite shut out,
A hard, dull bitterness of cold,
That checked, mid-vein, the circling race
Of lifeblood in the sharpened face,
The coming of the snowstorm told.
The wind blew east: we heard the roar
Of Ocean on his wintry shore,
And felt the strong pulse throbbing there
Beat with low rhythm our inland air.

Unwarmed by any sunset light
The gray day darkened into night,

SNOW-BOUND

A night made hoary with the swarm
And whirl-dance of the blinding storm,
As zigzag, wavering to and fro,
Crossed and recrossed the winged snow:
And ere the early bedtime came
The white drift piled the window frame,
And through the glass the clothesline posts
Looked in like tall and sheeted ghosts.

So all night long the storm roared on:
The morning broke without a sun;
In tiny spherule traced with lines
Of Nature's geometric signs,
In starry flake and pellicle,
All day the hoary meteor fell;
And, when the second morning shone,
We looked upon a world unknown,
On nothing we could call our own.
Around the glistening wonder bent
The blue walls of the firmament,
No cloud above, no earth below—
A universe of sky and snow!
The old familiar sights of ours
Took marvelous shapes; strange domes and towers
Rose up where sty or corncrib stood,
Or garden wall, or belt of wood;
A smooth white mound the brush pile showed,
A fenceless drift what once was road;
The bridle post an old man sat
With loose-flung coat and high cocked hat;
The wellcurb had a Chinese roof;
And even the long sweep, high aloof,

In its slant splendor, seemed to tell
Of Pisa's leaning miracle.

A prompt, decisive man, no breath
Our father wasted: "Boys, a path!"
Well pleased, (for when did farmer boy
Count such a summons less than joy?)
Our buskins on our feet we drew;
With mittened hands, and caps drawn low,
To guard our necks and ears from snow,
We cut the solid whiteness through.

THE WISE MEN

G. K. CHESTERTON
(1874–1936)

Step softly, under snow or rain,
To find the place where men can pray;
The way is all so very plain
That we may lose the way.

The world grows terrible and white,
And blinding white the breaking day;
We walked bewildered in the light,
For something is too large for sight,
And something much too plain to say.

Hark! Laughter like a lion wakes
To roar to the resounding plain.
And the whole heaven shouts and shakes,
For God Himself is born again,
And we are little children walking
Through the snow and rain.

THE BIRDS' CHRISTMAS CAROL

KATE DOUGLAS WIGGIN
(1856–1923)

This story, first published in 1887, was hugely popular in its day. Victorian writers portrayed the strength of the human spirit most often through sentimental, weepy stories of dying or orphaned children. The Birds' Christmas Carol *is no exception, but with its engaging characters it retains an enduring quality of wonder, goodness, and hope.*

1

A LITTLE SNOW BIRD

It was very early Christmas morning, and in the stillness of the dawn, with the soft snow falling on the housetops, a little child was born in the Bird household.

They had intended to name the baby Lucy, if it were a girl; but they had not expected her on Christmas morning, and a real Christmas baby was not to be lightly named—the whole family agreed in that.

They were consulting about it in the nursery. Mr. Bird said that he had assisted in naming the three boys, and that he should leave this matter entirely to Mrs. Bird; Donald wanted the child called "Dorothy," after a pretty, curly-haired girl who sat next him in school; Paul chose "Luella," for Luella was the nurse who had been with him during his whole babyhood, up to the time of his first trousers, and the name suggested all sorts of comfortable things. Uncle Jack said that the first girl should always be named for her mother, no matter how hideous the name happened to be.

Grandma said that she would prefer not to take any part in the discussion, and everybody suddenly remembered that Mrs. Bird had thought of naming the baby Lucy, for Grandma herself; and, while it would be indelicate for her to favor that name, it would be against human nature for her to suggest any other, under the circumstances.

Hugh, the "hitherto baby," if that is a possible term, sat in one corner and said nothing, but felt, in some mysterious way, that his nose was out of joint; for there was a newer baby now, a possibility he had never taken into consideration; and the "first girl," too—a still higher development of treason, which made him actually green with jealousy.

But it was too profound a subject to be settled then and there, on the spot; besides, Mamma had not been asked, and everybody felt it rather absurd, after all, to forestall a decree that was certain to be absolutely wise, just, and perfect.

The reason that the subject had been brought up at all so early in the day lay in the fact that Mrs. Bird never allowed her babies to go overnight unnamed. She was a person of so great decision of character that she would have blushed at such a thing; she said that to let blessed babies go dangling and dawdling about without names, for months and months, was enough to ruin them for life. She also said that if one could not make up one's mind in twenty-four hours it was a sign that—But I will not repeat the rest, as it might prejudice you against the most charming woman in the world.

So Donald took his new velocipede and went out to ride up and down the stone pavement and notch the shins of innocent people as they passed by, while Paul spun his musical top on the front steps.

But Hugh refused to leave the scene of action. He seated himself on the top stair in the hall, banged his head against the railing a few times, just by way of uncorking the vials of his wrath, and then subsided into gloomy silence, waiting to declare war if more "first girl babies" were thrust upon a family already surfeited with that unnecessary article.

Meanwhile dear Mrs. Bird lay in her room, weak, but safe and happy, with her sweet girl baby by her side and the heaven of motherhood opening again before her. Nurse was making gruel in the kitchen, and the room was dim and quiet. There was a cheerful open fire in the grate, but though the shutters were closed, the side windows that looked out on the Church of Our Savior, next door, were a little open.

Suddenly a sound of music poured out into the bright air and drifted into the chamber. It was the boy choir singing Christmas anthems. Higher and higher rose the clear, fresh voices, full of hope and cheer, as children's voices always are. Fuller and fuller grew the burst of melody as one glad strain fell upon another in joyful harmony:

Carol, brothers, carol,
Carol joyfully,
Carol the good tidings,
Carol merrily!
And pray a gladsome Christmas
For all your fellow-men:
Carol, brothers, carol,
Christmas Day again.

One verse followed another, always with the same sweet refrain:

And pray a gladsome Christmas
For all your fellow-men:
Carol, brothers, carol,
Christmas Day again.

Mrs. Bird thought, as the music floated in upon her gentle sleep, that she had slipped into heaven with her new baby, and that the angels were bidding them welcome. But the tiny bundle by her side stirred a little, and though it was scarcely more than the ruffling of a feather, she awoke; for the mother-ear is so close to the heart that it can hear the faintest whisper of a child.

She opened her eyes and drew the baby closer. It looked like a rose dipped in milk, she thought, this pink and white blossom of girlhood, or like a pink cherub, with its halo of pale yellow hair, finer than floss silk.

> Carol, brothers, carol,
> Carol joyfully,
> Carol the good tidings,
> Carol merrily!

The voices were brimming over with joy.

"Why, my baby," whispered Mrs. Bird in soft surprise, "I had forgotten what day it was. You are a little Christmas child, and we will name you 'Carol'—mother's Christmas Carol!"

"What!" said Mr. Bird, coming in softly and closing the door behind him.

"Why, Donald, don't you think 'Carol' is a sweet name for a Christmas baby? It came to me just a moment ago in the singing, as I was lying here half asleep and half awake."

"I think it is a charming name, dear heart, and sounds just like you, and I hope that, being a girl, this baby has some chance of being as lovely as her mother;"—at which speech from the baby's papa, Mrs. Bird, though she was as weak and tired as she could be, blushed with happiness.

And so Carol came by her name.

Of course, it was thought foolish by many people, though Uncle Jack declared laughingly that it was very strange if a whole family of Birds could not be indulged in a single Carol; and Grandma, who adored the child, thought the name much more appropriate than Lucy, but was glad that people would probably think it short for Caroline.

Perhaps because she was born in holiday time, Carol was a very happy baby. Or course, she was too tiny to understand the joy of Christmas-tide, but people say there is everything in a good beginning, and she may have breathed in unconsciously the fragrance of evergreens and holiday dinners; while the peals of sleigh-bells and the laughter of happy children may have fallen upon her baby ears and wakened in them a glad surprise at the merry world she had come to live in.

Her cheeks and lips were as red as hollyberries; her hair was for all the world the color of Christmas candle-flame; her eyes were bright as stars; her laugh like a chime of Christmas bells, and her tiny hands forever outstretched in giving.

Such a generous little creature you never saw! A spoonful of bread and milk had always to be taken by Mamma or nurse before Carol could enjoy her supper; whatever bit of cake or sweetmeat found its way into her pretty fingers was straightway broken in half to be shared with Donald, Paul, or Hugh; and when they made believe nibble the morsel with affected enjoyment, she would clap her hands and crow with delight.

"Why does she do it?" asked Donald thoughtfully. "None of us boys ever did."

"I hardly know," said Mamma, catching her darling to her heart, "except that she is a little Christmas child, and so she has a tiny share of the blessedest birthday the world ever knew!"

2

Drooping Wings

It was December, ten years later.

Carol had seen nine Christmas trees lighted on her birthdays, one after another; nine times she had assisted in the holiday festivities of the household, though in her babyhood her share of the gaieties was somewhat limited.

For five years, certainly, she had hidden presents for Mamma and Papa in their own bureau drawers, and harbored a number of secrets sufficiently large to burst a baby brain, had it not been for the relief gained by whispering them all to Mamma, at night, when she was in her crib, a proceeding which did not in the least lessen the value of a secret in her innocent mind.

For five years she had heard " 'Twas the night before Christmas," and hung up a scarlet stocking many sizes too large for her, and pinned a sprig of holly on her little white nightgown, to show Santa Claus that she was a "truly" Christmas child, and dreamed of fur-coated saints and toy-packs and reindeer, and wished everybody a "Merry Christmas" before it was light in the morning, and lent every one of her new toys to the neighbors' children before noon, and eaten turkey and plum-pudding, and gone to bed at night in a trance of happiness at the day's pleasures.

Donald was away at college now. Paul and Hugh were great manly fellows, taller than their mother. Papa Bird had gray hairs in his whiskers; and Grandma, God bless her, had been four Christmases in heaven.

But Christmas in the Birds' Nest was scarcely as merry now as it used to be in the bygone years, for the little child, that once brought such an added blessing to the day, lay month after month a patient, helpless invalid, in the room where she was born. She had never been very strong in body, and it was with a pang of terror her mother and father noticed, soon after she was five years old, that she began to limp, ever so slightly; to complain too often of weariness, and to nestle close to her mother, saying she "would rather not go out to play, please." The illness was slight at first, and hope was always stirring in Mrs. Bird's heart. "Carol would feel stronger in the summertime"; or, "She would be better when she had spent a year in the country"; or, "She would outgrow it"; or, "They would try a new physician"; but by and by it came to be all too sure that no physician save One could make Carol strong again, and that no "summertime" nor "country air," unless it were the everlasting summertime in a heavenly country, could bring back the little girl to health.

The cheeks and lips that were once as red as holly-berries faded to faint pink; the starlike eyes grew softer, for they often gleamed through tears; and the gay child-laugh, that had been like a chime of Christmas bells, gave place to a smile so lovely, so touching, so tender and patient, that it filled every corner of the house with a gentle radiance that might have come from the face of the Christ-child himself.

Love could do nothing; and when we have said that we have said all, for it is stronger than anything else in the whole wide world. Mr. and Mrs. Bird were talking it over one evening, when all the children were asleep. A famous physician had visited them that day, and told them that some time, it might be in one year, it might be in more, Carol would slip quietly off into heaven, whence she came.

"It is no use to close our eyes to it any longer," said Mr. Bird, as he paced up and down the library floor; "Carol will never be well again. It almost seems as if I could not bear it when I think of that loveliest child doomed to lie there day after day, and, what is still more, to suffer pain that we are helpless to keep away from her. Merry Christmas, indeed; it gets to be the saddest day in the year to me!" and poor Mr. Bird sank into a chair by the table, and buried his face in his hands to keep his wife from seeing the tears that would come in spite of all his efforts.

"But, Donald, dear," said sweet Mrs. Bird, with trembling voice, "Christmas Day may not be so merry with us as it used, but it is very happy, and that is better, and very blessed, and that is better yet. I suffer chiefly for Carol's sake, but I have almost given up being sorrowful for my own. I am too happy in the child, and I see too clearly what she has done for us and the other children. Donald and Paul and Hugh were three strong, willful, boisterous boys, but now you seldom see such tenderness, devotion, thought for others, and self-denial in lads of their years. A quarrel or a hot word is almost unknown in this house, and why? Carol would hear it, and it would distress her, she is so full of love and goodness. The boys study with all their might and main. Why? Partly, at least, because they like to teach Carol, and amuse her by telling her what they read. When the seamstress comes, she likes to sew in Miss Carol's room, because there she forgets her own troubles, which, Heaven knows, are sore enough! And as for me, Donald, I am a better woman every day for Carol's sake; I have to be her eyes, ears, feet, hands, her strength, her hope; and she, my own little child, is my example!"

"I was wrong, dear heart," said Mr. Bird more cheerfully; "we will try not to repine, but to rejoice instead, that we have an 'angel of the house.' "

"And as for her future," Mrs. Bird went on, "I think we need not be over-anxious. I feel as if she did not belong altogether to us, but that when she has done what God sent her for, He will take her back to Himself—and it may not be very long!" Here it was poor Mrs. Bird's turn to break down, and Mr. Bird's turn to comfort her.

3

THE BIRDS' NEST

Carol herself knew nothing of motherly tears and fatherly anxieties; she lived on peacefully in the room where she was born.

But you never would have known that room; for Mr. Bird had a great deal of money, and though he felt sometimes as if he wanted to throw it all in the sea, since it could not buy a strong body for his little girl, yet he was glad to make the place she lived in just as beautiful as it could be.

The room had been extended by the building of a large addition that hung out over the garden below, and was so filled with windows that it might have been a conservatory. The ones on the side were thus still nearer the Church of Our Savior than they used to be; those in front looked out on the beautiful harbor, and those in the back commanded a view of nothing in particular but a narrow alley; nevertheless, they were pleasantest of all to Carol, for the Ruggles family lived in the alley, and the nine little, middle-sized, and big Ruggles children were a source of inexhaustible interest.

The shutters could all be opened and Carol could take a real sun-bath in this lovely glass house, or they could all be closed when the dear head ached or the dear eyes were tired. The carpet was of soft gray, with clusters of green bay and holly leaves. The furniture was of white wood, on which an artist had painted snow scenes and Christmas trees and groups of merry children ringing bells and singing carols.

Donald had made a pretty, polished shelf, and screwed it on the outside of the footboard, and the boys always kept this full of blooming plants, which they changed from time to time; the head-board, too, had a bracket on either side, where there were pots of maidenhair ferns.

Lovebirds and canaries hung in their golden houses in the windows, and they, poor caged things, could hop as far from their wooden perches as Carol could venture from her little white bed.

On one side of the room was a bookcase filled with hundreds—yes, I mean it—with hundreds and hundreds of books; books with gay-colored pictures, books without; books with black and white outline sketches, books with none at all; books with verses, books with stories; books that made children laugh, and some, only a few, that made them cry; books with words of one syllable for tiny boys and girls, and books with words of fearful length to puzzle wise ones.

This was Carol's "Circulating Library." Every Saturday she chose ten books, jotting their names down in a diary; into these she slipped cards that said:

> Please keep this book two weeks and read it.
> With love, CAROL BIRD.

Then Mrs. Bird stepped into her carriage and took the ten books to the Children's Hospital, and brought home ten others that she had left there the fortnight before.

This was a source of great happiness; for some of the hospital children that were old enough to print or write, and were strong enough to do it, wrote Carol sweet little letters about the books, and she answered them, and they grew to be friends. (It is very funny, but you do not always have to see people to love them. Just think about it, and tell me if it isn't so.)

There was a high wainscoting of wood about the room, and on top of this, in a narrow gilt framework, ran a row of illuminated pictures, illustrating fairy tales, all in dull blue and gold and scarlet and silver. From the door to the closet there was the story of "The Fair One with Golden Locks"; from closet to bookcase, ran "Puss in Boots"; from bookcase to fireplace, was "Jack the Giant-killer"; and on the other side of the room were "Hop o' my Thumb," "The Sleeping Beauty," and "Cinderella."

Then there was a great closet full of beautiful things to wear, but they were all dressing-gowns and slippers and shawls; and there were drawers full of toys and games, but they were such as you could play with on your lap. There were no ninepins, nor balls, nor bows and arrows, nor bean bags, nor tennis rackets; but, after all, other children needed these more than Carol Bird, for she was always happy and contented, whatever she had or whatever she lacked; and after the room had been made so lovely for her, on her eighth Christmas, she always called herself, in fun, a "Bird of Paradise."

On these particular December days she was happier than usual, for Uncle Jack was coming from England to spend the holidays. Dear, funny, jolly, loving, wise Uncle Jack, who came every two or three years, and brought so much joy with him that the world looked as black as a thundercloud for a week after he went away again.

The mail had brought this letter:

London, November 28, 188—.

Wish you merry Christmas, you dearest birdlings in America! Preen your feathers, and stretch the Birds' nest a trifle, if you please, and let Uncle Jack in for the holidays. I am coming with such a trunk full of treasures that you'll have to borrow the stockings of Barnum's Giant and Giantess; I am coming to squeeze a certain little lady-bird until she cries for mercy; I am coming to see if I can find a boy to take care of a black pony that I bought lately. It's the strangest thing I ever knew; I've hunted all over Europe, and can't find a boy to suit me! I'll tell you why. I've set my heart on finding one with a dimple in his chin, because this pony particularly likes dimples! ["Hurrah!" cried Hugh; "bless my dear dimple; I'll never be ashamed of it again."]

Please drop a note to the clerk of the weather, and have a good, rousing snowstorm—say on the twenty-second. None of your meek, gentle, nonsensical, shilly-shallying snow-storms; not the sort where the flakes float lazily down from the sky as if they didn't care whether they ever got here or not and then melt away as soon as they touch the earth, but a regular businesslike whizzing, whirring, blurring, cutting snowstorm, warranted to freeze and stay on!

I should like rather a LARGE Christmas tree, if it's convenient: not one of those "sprigs," five or six feet high, that you used to have three or four years ago, when the birdlings were not fairly feathered out; but a tree of some size. Set it up in the garret, if necessary, and then we can cut a hole in the roof if the tree chances to be too high for the room.

Tell Bridget to begin to fatten a turkey. Tell her that by the twentieth of December the turkey must not be able to stand on its legs for fat, and then on the next three days she must allow it to recline easily on its side, and stuff it to bursting. (One ounce of stuffing beforehand is worth a pound afterwards.)

The pudding must be unusually huge, and darkly, deeply, lugubriously blue in color. It must be stuck so full of plums that the pudding itself will ooze out into the pan and not be brought on to the table at all. I expect to be there by the twentieth, to manage these little things myself—remembering it is the early Bird that catches the worm—but give you the instructions in case I should be delayed.

And Carol must decide on the size of the tree—she knows best, she was a Christmas child; and she must plead for the snowstorm—the "clerk of the weather" may pay some attention to her; and she must look up the boy with the dimple for me—she's likelier to find him than I am, this minute. She must advise about the turkey, and Bridget must bring the pudding to her bedside and let her drop every separate plum into it and stir it once for luck, or I'll not eat a single slice—for Carol is the dearest part of Christmas to Uncle Jack, and he'll have none of it without her. She is better than all the turkeys and puddings and apples and spare-ribs and wreaths and garlands and mistletoe and stockings and chimneys and sleigh-bells in Christendom! She is the very sweetest Christmas Carol that was ever written, said, sung, or chanted, and I am coming as fast as ships and railway trains can carry me, to tell her so.

Carol's joy knew no bounds. Mr. and Mrs. Bird laughed like children and kissed each other for sheer delight, and when the boys heard it they simply whooped like wild Indians; until the Ruggles family, whose back yard joined their garden, gathered at the door and wondered what was "up" in the big house.

4

BIRDS OF A FEATHER FLOCK TOGETHER

Uncle Jack did really come on the twentieth. He was not detained by business, nor did he get left behind nor snowed up, as frequently happens in stories, and in real life too, I am afraid. The snowstorm came also; and the turkey nearly died a natural and premature death from overeating. Donald came, too; Donald, with a line of down upon his upper lip, and Greek and Latin on his tongue, and stores of knowledge in his handsome head, and stories—bless me, you couldn't turn over a chip without reminding Donald of something that happened "at college." One or the other was always at Carol's bedside, for they fancied her paler than she used to be, and they could not bear her out of sight. It was Uncle Jack, though, who sat beside her in the winter twilights. The room was quiet, and almost dark, save for the snow-light outside, and the flickering flame of the fire, that danced over the "Sleeping Beauty's" face and touched the Fair One's golden locks with ruddier glory. Carol's hand (all too thin and white these latterdays) lay close clasped in Uncle Jack's, and they talked together quietly of many, many things.

"I want to tell you all about my plans for Christmas this year, Uncle Jack," said Carol, on the first evening of his visit, "because it will be the loveliest one I ever had. The boys laugh at me for caring so much about it; but it isn't altogether because it is Christmas, nor because it is my birthday; but long, long ago, when I first began to be ill, I used to think, the first thing when I waked on Christmas morning, 'Today is Christ's birthday—*and mine!*' I did not put the words close together, you know, because that made it seem too bold; but I first said, 'Christ's birthday,' out loud, and then, in a minute, softly to myself—*'and mine!* Christ's birthday—*and mine!'* And so I do not quite feel about Christmas as other girls do. Mamma says she supposes that ever so many other children have been born on that day. I often wonder where they are, Uncle Jack, and whether it is a dear thought to them, too, or whether I am so much in bed, and so often alone, that it means more to me. Oh, I do hope that none of them are poor, or cold, or hungry; and I wish—I wish they were all as happy as I, because they are really my little brothers and sisters. Now, Uncle Jack dear, I am going to try and make somebody happy every single Christmas that I live, and this year it is to be the 'Ruggleses in the rear.' "

"That large and interesting brood of children in the little house at the end of the back garden?"

"Yes; isn't it nice to see so many together?—and, Uncle Jack, why do the big families always live in the small houses, and the small families in the big houses? We ought to call them the Ruggles children, of course; but Donald began talking of them as the 'Ruggleses in the rear,' and Papa and Mamma took it up, and now we cannot seem to help it. The house was built for Mr. Carter's coachman, but Mr. Carter lives in Europe, and the gentleman who rents his place for him doesn't care what happens to it, and so this poor family came to live there. When they first moved in, I used to sit in my window and watch them play in their back yard; they are so strong, and jolly, and good-natured;—and then, one day, I had a terrible headache, and Donald asked them if they would please not scream quite so loud, and they explained that they were having a game of circus, but that they would change and play 'Deaf and Dumb Asylum' all the afternoon."

"Ha, ha, ha!" laughed Uncle Jack, "what an obliging family, to be sure!"

"Yes, we all thought it very funny, and I smiled at them from the window when I was well enough to be up again. Now, Sarah Maud comes to her door when the children come home from school, and if Mamma nods her head, 'Yes,' that means 'Carol is very well,' and then you ought to hear the little Ruggleses yell,—I believe they try to see how much noise they can make; but if Mamma shakes her head, 'No,' they always play at quiet games. Then, one day, 'Cary,' my pet canary, flew out of her cage, and Peter Ruggles caught her and brought her back, and I had him up here in my room to thank him."

"Is Peter the oldest?"

"No; Sarah Maud is the oldest—she helps do the washing; and Peter is the next. He is a dressmaker's boy."

"And which is the pretty little red-haired girl?"

"That's Kitty."

"And the fat youngster?"

"Baby Larry."

"And that—most freckled one?"

"Now, don't laugh—that's Peoria."

"Carol, you are joking."

"No, really, Uncle dear. She was born in Peoria; that's all."

"And is the next boy Oshkosh?"

"No," laughed Carol, "the others are Susan, and Clement, and Eily, and Cornelius; they all look exactly alike, except that some of them have more freckles than the others."

"How did you ever learn all their names?"

"Why, I have what I call a 'window-school.' It is too cold now; but in warm weather I am wheeled out on my balcony, and the Ruggleses climb up and walk along our garden fence, and sit down on the roof of our carriage-house. That brings them quite near, and I tell them stories. On Thanksgiving Day they came up for a few minutes,—it was quite warm at eleven o'clock,—and we told each other what we had to be thankful for; but they gave such queer answers that Papa had to run away for fear of laughing; and I couldn't understand them very well. Susan was thankful for *'trunks,'* of all things in the world; Cornelius, for 'horse-cars'; Kitty, for 'pork steak'; while Clem, who is very quiet, brightened up when I came to him, and said he was thankful for *'his lame puppy.'* Wasn't that pretty?"

"It might teach some of us a lesson, mightn't it, little girl?"

"That's what Mamma said. Now I'm going to give this whole Christmas to the Ruggleses; and, Uncle Jack, I earned part of the money myself."

"You, my bird; how?"

"Well, you see, it could not be my own, own Christmas if Papa gave me all the money, and I thought to really keep Christ's birthday I ought to do something of my very own; and so I talked with Mamma. Of course she thought of something lovely; she always does: Mamma's head is just brimming over with lovely thoughts,—all I have to do is ask, and out pops the very one I want. This thought was to let her write down, just as I told her, a description of how a child lived in her own room for three years, and what she did to amuse herself; and we sent it to a magazine and got twenty-five dollars for it. Just think!"

"Well, well," cried Uncle Jack, "my little girl a real author! And what are you going to do with this wonderful 'own' money of yours?"

"I shall give the nine Ruggleses a grand Christmas dinner here in this very room—that will be Papa's contribution,—and afterwards a beautiful Christmas tree, fairly blooming with presents—that will be my part; for I have another way of adding to my twenty-five dollars, so that I can buy nearly anything I choose. I should like it very much if you would sit at the head of the table, Uncle Jack, for nobody could ever be frightened of you, you dearest, dearest, dearest thing that ever was! Mamma is going to help us, but Papa and the boys are going to eat together downstairs for fear of making the little Ruggleses shy; and after we've had a merry time with the tree we can open my window and all listen together to the music at the evening church-service, if it comes before the children go. I have written a letter to the organist, and asked him if I might have the two songs I like best. Will you see if it is all right?"

BIRDS' NEST, December 21, 188—.

DEAR MR. WILKIE,—I am the little girl who lives next door to the church, and, as I seldom go out, the music on practice days and Sundays is one of my greatest pleasures.

I want to know if you can have "Carol, Brothers, Carol," on Christmas night, and if the boy who sings "My Ain Countree" so beautifully may please sing that too. I think it is the loveliest thing in the world, but it always makes me cry; doesn't it you?

If it isn't too much trouble, I hope they can sing them both quite early, as after ten o'clock I may be asleep.

Yours respectfully,
CAROL BIRD

P.S.—The reason I like "Carol, Brothers, Carol," is because the choir-boys sang it eleven years ago, the morning I was born, and put it into Mamma's head to call me Carol. She didn't remember then that my other name would be Bird, because she was half asleep, and could only think of one thing at a time. Donald says if I had been born on the Fourth of July they would have named me "Independence," or if on the twenty-second of February, "Georgina," or even "Cherry," like Cherry in "Martin Chuzzlewit"; but I like my own name and birthday best.

Yours truly,
CAROL BIRD

Uncle Jack thought the letter quite right, and did not even smile at her telling the organist so many family items.

The days flew by as they always fly in holiday time, and it was Christmas Eve before anybody knew it. The family festival was quiet and very pleasant, but almost overshadowed by the grander preparations for the next day. Carol and Elfrida, her pretty German nurse, had ransacked books, and introduced so many plans, and plays, and customs, and merry-makings from Germany, and Holland, and England, and a dozen other countries, that you would scarcely have known how or where you were keeping Christmas. Even the dog and the cat had enjoyed their celebration under Carol's direction. Each had a tiny table with a lighted candle in the center, and a bit of Bologna sausage placed very near it; and everybody laughed till the tears stood in their eyes to see Villikins and Dinah struggle to nibble the sausages, and at the same time to evade the candle flame. Villikins barked, and sniffed, and howled in impatience, and after many vain attempts succeeded in dragging off the prize, though he singed his nose in doing it. Dinah, meanwhile, watched him placidly, her delicate nostrils quivering with expectation, and, after all excitement had subsided, walked with dignity to the table, her beautiful gray satin tail sweeping behind her, and, calmly putting up one velvet paw, drew the sausage gently down, and walked out of the room without turning a hair, so to speak. Elfrida had scattered handfuls of seed over the snow in the garden, that the wild birds might have a comfortable breakfast next morning, and had stuffed bundles of dry grasses in the fireplaces, so that the reindeer of Santa Claus could refresh themselves after their long gallops across country. This was really only done for fun, but it pleased Carol.

And when, after dinner, the whole family had gone to the church to see the Christmas decorations, Carol limped out on her slender crutches, and with Elfrida's help, placed all the family boots in a row in the upper hall. That was to keep the dear ones from quarreling all through the year. There were Papa's stout top boots; Mamma's pretty buttoned shoes next; then Uncle Jack's, Donald's, Paul's, and Hugh's; and at the end of the line her own little white worsted slippers. Last, and sweetest of all, like the children in Austria, she put a lighted candle in her window to guide the dear Christ-child, lest he should stumble in the dark night as he passed up the deserted street. This done, she dropped into bed, a rather tired, but very happy Christmas fairy.

5

Some Other Birds Are Taught to Fly

Before the earliest Ruggles could wake and toot his five-cent tin horn, Mrs. Ruggles was up and stirring about the house, for it was a gala day in the family. Gala day! I should think so! Were not her nine "childern" invited to a dinner-party at the great house, and weren't they going to sit down free and equal with the mightiest in the land? She had been preparing for this grand occasion ever since the receipt of Carol Bird's invitation, which, by the way, had been speedily enshrined in an old photograph frame and hung under the looking-glass in the most prominent place in the kitchen, where it stared the occasional visitor directly in the eye, and made him livid with envy:

Birds' Nest, December 17, 188—.

Dear Mrs. Ruggles,—I am going to have a dinner-party on Christmas Day, and would like to have all your children come. I want them every one, please, from Sarah Maud to Baby Larry. Mamma says dinner will be at half past five, and the Christmas tree at seven; so you may expect them home at nine o'clock. Wishing you a Merry Christmas and a Happy New Year, I am

Yours truly,
CAROL BIRD

Breakfast was on the table promptly at seven o'clock, and there was very little of it, too; for it was an excellent day for short rations, though Mrs. Ruggles heaved a sigh as she reflected that the boys, with their India-rubber stomachs, would be just as hungry the day after the dinner-party as if they had never had any at all.

As soon as the scanty meal was over, she announced the plan of the campaign: "Now, Susan, you an' Kitty wash up the dishes; an' Peter, can't yer spread up the beds, so 't I can git ter cuttin' out Larry's new suit? I ain't satisfied with his clo'es, an' I thought in the night of a way to make him a dress out o' my old red plaid shawl—kind o' Scotch style, yer know, with the fringe 't the bottom.—Eily, you go find the comb and take the snarls out the fringe, that's a lady! You little young ones clear out from under foot! Clem, you and Con hop into bed with Larry while I wash yer underflannins; 't won't take long to dry 'em.—Yes, I know it's bothersome, but yer can't go int' s'ciety 'thout takin' some trouble, 'n' anyhow I couldn't git round to 'em last night.—Sarah Maud, I think 't would be perfeckly han'som' if you ripped them brass buttons off your uncle's *po*liceman's coat 'n' sewed 'em in a row up the front o' yer green skirt. Susan, you must iron out yours 'n' Kitty's apurns; 'n' there, I come mighty near forgettin' Peory's stockin's! I counted the whole lot last night when I was washin' of 'em, 'n' there ain't but nineteen anyhow yer fix 'em, 'n' no nine pairs of mates nohow; 'n' I ain't goin' ter have my childern wear odd stockin's to a dinner-comp'ny, fetched up as I was!—Eily, can't you run out and ask Mis' Cullen ter lend me a pair o' stockin's for

Peory, 'n' tell her if she will, Peory'll give Jim half her candy when she gets home. Won't yer, Peory?"

Peoria was young and greedy, and thought the remedy so out of all proportion to the disease, that she set up a deafening howl at the projected bargain—a howl so rebellious and so entirely out of season that her mother started in her direction with flashing eye and uplifted hand; but she let it fall suddenly, saying, "No, I vow I won't lick ye Christmas Day, if yer drive me crazy; but speak up smart, now, 'n' say whether yer'd ruther give Jim Cullen half yer candy or go bare-legged ter the party?" The matter being put so plainly, Peoria collected her faculties, dried her tears, and chose the lesser evil, Clem having hastened the decision by an affectionate wink, that meant he'd go halves with her on his candy.

"That's a lady!" cried her mother. "Now, you young ones that ain't doin' nothin', play all yer want ter before noontime, for after ye git through eatin' at twelve o'clock me 'n' Sarah Maud's goin' ter give yer sech a washin' 'n' combin' 'n' dressin' as yer never had before 'n' never will agin likely, 'n' then I'm going to set yer down 'n' give yer two solid hours trainin' in manners; 'n' 'twon't be no foolin' neither."

"All we've got ter do's go eat!" grumbled Peter.

"Well, that's enough," responded his mother; "there's more'n one way of eatin', let me tell yer, 'n' you've got a heap ter learn about it, Peter Ruggles. Land sakes, I wish you children could see the way I was fetched up to eat. I never took a meal o' vittles in the kitchen before I married Ruggles; but yer can't keep up that style with nine young ones 'n' yer Pa always off ter sea."

The big Ruggleses worked so well, and the little Ruggleses kept from "under foot" so successfully, that by one o'clock, nine complete toilets were laid out in solemn grandeur on the beds. I say, "complete"; but I do not know whether they would be called so in the best society. The law of compensation had been well applied: he that had necktie had no cuffs; she that had sash had no handkerchief, and vice versa; but they all had shoes and a certain amount of clothing, such as it was, the outside layer being in every case quite above criticism.

"Now, Sarah Maud," said Mrs. Ruggles, her face shining with excitement, "everything's red up an' we can begin. I've got a boiler 'n' a kettle 'n' a pot o' hot water. Peter, you go into the back bedroom, 'n' I'll take Susan, Kitty, Peory, 'n' Cornelius; 'n' Sarah Maud, you take Clem, 'n' Eily, 'n' Larry, one at a time. Scrub 'em 'n' rinse 'em, or, 't any rate git's fur's yer can with 'em, and then I'll finish 'em off while you do yerself."

Sarah Maud couldn't have scrubbed with any more decision and force if she had been doing floors, and the little Ruggleses bore it bravely, not from natural heroism, but for the joy that was set before them. Not being satisfied, however, with the "tone" of their complexions, and feeling that the number of freckles to the square inch was too many to be tolerated in the highest social circles, she wound up operations by applying a little Bristol brick from the knife-board, which served as the proverbial "last straw," from under which the little Ruggleses issued rather red and raw and out of temper. When the clock struck four they were all clothed, and most of them in their right minds, ready for those last touches that always take the most time.

Kitty's red hair was curled in thirty-four ringlets, Sarah Maud's was braided in one pig-tail, and Susan's and Eily's in two braids apiece, while Peoria's resisted all advances in the shape of hair oils and stuck out straight on all sides, like that of the Circassian girl of the circus—so Clem said; and he was sent into the bedroom for it, too, from whence he was dragged out forgivingly, by Peoria herself, five minutes later. Then, exciting moment, came linen collars for some and neckties and bows for others—a magnificent green glass breastpin was sewed into Peter's purple necktie—and

Eureka! the Ruggleses were dressed, and Solomon in all his glory was not arrayed like one of these!

A row of seats was then formed directly through the middle of the kitchen. Of course, there were not quite chairs enough for ten, since the family had rarely wanted to sit down all at once, somebody always being out or in bed, or otherwise engaged, but the wood-box and the coal-hod finished out the line nicely, and nobody thought of grumbling. The children took their places according to age, Sarah Maud at the head and Larry on the coal-hod, and Mrs. Ruggles seated herself in front, surveying them proudly as she wiped the sweat of honest toil from her brow.

"Well," she exclaimed, "if I do say so as shouldn't, I never seen a cleaner, more stylish mess o' childern in my life! I do wish Ruggles could look at ye for a minute!—Larry Ruggles, how many times have I got ter tell yer not ter keep pullin' at yer sash? Haven't I told yer if it comes ontied, yer waist 'n' skirt'll part comp'ny in the middle, 'n' then where'll yer be?—Now look me in the eye, all of yer! I've of'en told yer what kind of a family the McGrills was. I've got reason to be proud, goodness knows! Your uncle is on the *po*lice force o' New York City; you can take up the paper most any day an' see his name printed right out—James McGrill,—'n' I can't have my childern fetched up common, like some folks'; when they go out they've got to have clo'es, and learn to act decent! Now I want ter see how yer goin' ter behave when yer git there to-night. 'Tain't so awful easy as you think 'tis. Let's start in at the beginnin' 'n' act out the whole business. Pile into the bedroom, there, every last one o' ye, 'n' show me how yer goin' to go int' the parlor. This'll be the parlor, 'n' I'll be Mis' Bird."

The youngsters hustled into the next room in high glee, and Mrs. Ruggles drew herself up in the chair with an infinitely haughty and purse-proud expression that much better suited a descendant of the McGrills than modest Mrs. Bird.

The bedroom was small, and there presently ensued such a clatter that you would have thought a herd of wild cattle had broken loose. The door opened, and they straggled in, all the younger ones giggling, with Sarah Maud at the head, looking as if she had been caught in the act of stealing sheep; while Larry, being last in line, seemed to think the door a sort of gate of heaven which would be shut in his face if he didn't get there in time; accordingly he struggled ahead of his elders and disgraced himself by tumbling in head foremost.

Mrs. Ruggles looked severe. "There, I knew yer'd do it in some sech fool way! Now go in there and try it over again, every last one o' ye, 'n' if Larry can't come in on two legs he can stay ter home,—'d yer hear?"

The matter began to assume a graver aspect; the little Ruggleses stopped giggling and backed into the bedroom, issuing presently with lock step, Indian file, a scared and hunted expression on every countenance.

"No, no, no!" cried Mrs. Ruggles, in despair. "That's worse yet; yer look for all the world like a gang o' pris'ners! There ain't no style ter that: spread out more, can't yer, 'n' act kind o' carelesslike—nobody's goin' ter kill ye! That ain't what a dinner-party is!"

The third time brought deserved success, and the pupils took their seats in the row. "Now, yer know," said Mrs. Ruggles impressively, "there ain't enough decent hats to go round, 'n' if there was I don' know's I'd let yer wear 'em, for the boys would never think to take 'em off when they got inside, for they never do—but anyhow, there ain't enough good ones. Now, look me in the eye. You're only goin' jest round the corner; you needn't wear no hats, none of yer, 'n' when yer get int' the parlor, 'n' they ask yer ter lay off yer hats, Sarah Maud must speak up 'n' say it was sech a pleasant evenin' 'n' sech a short walk that yer left yer hats to home. Now, can yer remember?

All the little Ruggleses shouted, "Yes, marm!" in chorus.

"What have *you* got ter do with it?" demanded their mother; "did I tell *you* to say it? Warn't I talkin' ter Sarah Maud?"

The little Ruggleses hung their diminished heads. "Yes, marm," they piped, more discreetly.

"Now we won't leave nothin' to chance; git up, all of ye, an' try it.—Speak up, Sarah Maud."

Sarah Maud's tongue clove to the roof of her mouth.

"Quick!"

"Ma thought—it was—sech a pleasant hat that we'd—we'd better leave our short walk to home," recited Sarah Maud, in an agony of mental effort.

This was too much for the boys. An earthquake of suppressed giggles swept all along the line.

"Oh, whatever shall I do with yer?" moaned the unhappy mother; "I s'pose I've got to learn it to yer!"—which she did, word for word, until Sarah Maud thought she could stand on her head and say it backwards.

"Now, Cornelius, what are *you* goin' ter say ter make yerself good comp'ny?"

"Do? Me? Dunno!" said Cornelius, turning pale, with unexpected responsibility.

"Well, ye ain't goin' to set there like a bump on a log 'thout sayin' a word ter pay for yer vittles, air ye? Ask Mis' Bird how she's feelin' this evenin', or if Mr. Bird's hevin' a busy season, or how this kind o' weather agrees with him, or somethin' like that.—Now we'll make b'lieve we've got ter the dinner—that won't be so hard, 'cause yer'll have somethin' to do—it's awful bothersome to stan' round and act stylish.—If they have napkins, Sarah Maud down to Peory may put 'em in their laps, 'n' the rest of ye can tuck 'em in yer necks. Don't eat with yer fingers—don't grab no vittles off one 'nother's plates; don't reach out for nothin', but wait till yer asked, 'n' if you never *git* asked don't git up and grab it.—Don't spill nothin' on the tablecloth, or like's not Mis' Bird'll send yer away from the table—'n' I hope she will if yer do! (Susan! keep your handkerchief in your lap where Peory can borry it if she needs it, 'n' I hope she'll know when she does need it, though I don't expect it.) Now we'll try a few things ter see how they'll go! Mr. Clement, do you eat cramb'ry sarse?"

"Bet yer life!" cried Clem, who in the excitement of the moment had not taken in the idea exactly and had mistaken this for an ordinary bosom-of-the-family question.

"Clement McGrill Ruggles, do you mean to tell me that you'd say that to a dinner-party? I'll give ye one more chance, Mr. Clement, will you take some of the cramb'ry?"

"Yes, marm, thank ye kindly, if you happen ter have any handy."

"Very good, indeed! But they won't give yer two tries to-night—yer just remember that!—Miss Peory, do you speak for white or dark meat?"

"I ain't perticler as ter color—anything that nobody else wants will suit me," answered Peory with her best air.

"First-rate! Nobody could speak more genteel than that. Miss Kitty, will you have hard or soft sarse with your pudden?"

"Hard or soft? Oh! A little of both, if you please, an' I'm much obliged," said Kitty, bowing with decided ease and grace; at which all the other Ruggleses pointed the finger of shame at her, and Peter *grunted* expressively, that their meaning might not be mistaken.

"You just stop your gruntin', Peter Ruggles; that warn't greedy, that was all right. I wish I could git it inter your heads that it ain't so much what yer say, as the way you say it. And don't keep starin' cross-eyed at your necktie pin, or I'll take it out 'n' sew it on to Clem or Cornelius: Sarah Maud'll keep her eye on it, 'n' if it turns broken side out she'll tell yer. Gracious! I shouldn't think you'd ever seen nor worn no jool'ry in your life.—Eily, you an' Larry's too little to train, so you just look at the rest an' do's they do, 'n' the

Lord have mercy on ye 'n' help ye to act decent! Now, is there anything more ye'd like to practice?"

"If yer tell me one more thing, I can't set up an' eat," said Peter gloomily; "I'm so cram full o' manners now I'm ready ter bust, 'thout no dinner at all."

"Me too," chimed in Cornelius.

"Well, I'm sorry for yer both," rejoined Mrs. Ruggles sarcastically; "if the 'mount o' manners yer've got on hand now troubles ye, you're dreadful easy hurt! Now, Sarah Maud, after dinner, about once in so often, you must git up 'n' say, "I guess we'd better be goin', 'n' if they say, 'Oh, no, set a while longer,' yer can set; but if they don't say nothin' you've got ter get up 'n' go.—Now hev yer got that int' yer head?"

"About once in so often!" Could any words in the language be fraught with more terrible and wearing uncertainty?

"Well," answered Sarah Maud mournfully, "seems as if this whole dinner-party set right square on top o' me! Mebbe I could manage my own manners, but to manage nine mannerses is worse'n staying to home!"

"Oh, don't fret," said her mother, good-naturedly, now that the lesson was over; "I guess you'll git along. I wouldn't mind if folks would only say, 'Oh, childern will be childern'; but they won't. They'll say, 'Land o' Goodness, who fetched them childern up?' —It's quarter past five, 'n' yer can go now:—remember 'bout the hats—don't all talk ter once—Susan, lend yer han'k'chief ter Peory—Peter, don't keep screwin' yer scarf-pin—Cornelius, hold yer head up straight—Sarah Maud, don't take yer eyes off o' Larry, 'n' Larry you keep holt o' Sarah Maud 'n' do jest as she says—'n' whatever you do, all of yer, never forgit for one second that yer mother was a McGrill."

6

When the Pie Was Opened, the Birds Began to Sing!

The children went out of the back door quietly, and were presently lost to sight, Sarah Maud slipping and stumbling along absent-mindedly, as she recited rapidly under her breath, "Itwassuchapleasantevenin'n'suchashortwalk,thatwethoughtwe'dleaveourhatstohome.— Itwassuchapleasantevenin'n'suchashortwalk, thatwe-thoughtwe'dleaveourhatsto home."

Peter rang the door-bell, and presently a servant admitted them, and, whispering something in Sarah's ear, drew her downstairs into the kitchen. The other Ruggleses stood in horror-stricken groups at the door closed behind their commanding officer; but there was no time for reflection, for a voice from above was heard, saying, "Come right upstairs, please!"

> Theirs not to make reply,
> Theirs not to reason why,
> Theirs but to do or die.

Accordingly they walked upstairs, and Elfrida, the nurse, ushered them into a room more splendid than anything they had ever seen. But, oh woe! where was Sarah Maud! and was it fate that Mrs. Bird should say, at once, "Did you lay your hats in the hall?" Peter felt himself elected by circumstance the head of the family, and, casting one imploring look at tongue-tied Susan, standing next him, said huskily, "It was so very pleasant—that—that—" "That we hadn't good hats enough to go 'round," put in little Susan, bravely, to help him out, and then froze with horror that the ill-fated words had slipped off her tongue.

However, Mrs. Bird said, pleasantly, "Of course you wouldn't wear hats such a short distance—I forgot when I asked. Now will you come right in to Miss Carol's room? She is so anxious to see you."

Just then Sarah Maud came up the back stairs, so radiant with joy from her secret interview with the cook that Peter could have pinched her with a clear conscience; and Carol gave them a joyful welcome. "But where is Baby Larry?" she cried, looking over the group with searching eye. "Didn't he come?"

"Larry! Larry!" Good gracious, where was Larry? They were all sure that he had come in with them, for Susan remembered scolding him for tripping over the doormat. Uncle Jack went into convulsions of laughter. "Are you sure there were nine of you?" he asked, merrily.

"I think so, sir," said Peoria, timidly; "but anyhow, there was Larry"; and she showed signs of weeping.

"Oh, well, cheer up!" cried Uncle Jack. "Probably he's not lost—only mislaid. I'll go and find him before you can say Jack Robinson!"

"I'll go, too, if you please, sir," said Sarah Maud, "for it was my place to mind him, an' if he's lost I can't relish my vittles!"

The other Ruggleses stood rooted to the floor. Was this a dinner-party, forsooth; and if so, why were such things ever spoken of as festive occasions?

Sarah Maud went out through the hall, calling, "Larry! Larry!" and without any interval of suspense a thin voice piped up from below, "Here I be!"

The truth was that Larry, being deserted by his natural guardian, dropped behind the rest, and wriggled into the hat-tree to wait for her, having no notion of walking unprotected into the jaws of a fashionable entertainment. Finding that she did not come, he tried to crawl from his refuge and call somebody, when—dark and dreadful ending to a tragic day—he found that he was too much intertwined with umbrellas and canes to move a single step. He was afraid to yell (when I have said this of Larry Ruggles I have pictured a state of helpless terror that ought to wring tears from every eye); and the sound of Sarah Maud's beloved voice, some seconds later, was like a strain of angel music in his ears. Uncle Jack dried his tears, carried him upstairs, and soon had him in breathless fits of laughter, while Carol so made the other Ruggleses forget themselves that they were presently talking like accomplished diners-out.

Carol's bed had been moved into the farthest corner of the room, and she was lying on the outside, dressed in a wonderful dressing-gown that looked like a fleecy cloud. Her golden hair fell in fluffy curls over her white forehead and neck, her cheeks flushed delicately, her eyes beamed with joy, and the children told their mother, afterwards, that she looked as beautiful as the angels in the picture books.

There was a great bustle behind a huge screen in another part of the room, and at half past five this was taken away, and the Christmas dinner-table stood revealed. What a wonderful sight it was to the poor little Ruggles children, who ate their sometimes scanty meals on the kitchen table! It blazed with tall colored candles, it gleamed with glass and silver, it blushed with flowers, it groaned with good things to eat; so it was not strange that the Ruggleses, forgetting altogether that their mother was a McGrill, shrieked in admiration of the fairy spectacle. But Larry's behavior was the most disgraceful, for he stood not upon the order of his going, but went at once for a high chair that pointed unmistakably to him, climbed up like a squirrel, gave a comprehensive look at the turkey, clapped his hands in ecstasy, rested his fat arms on the table, and cried with joy, "I beat the hull lot o' yer!" Carol laughed until she cried, giving orders, meanwhile,—"Uncle Jack, please sit at the head, Sarah Maud at the foot, and that will leave four on each side; Mamma is going to help Elfrida, so that the children need not look after each other, but just have a good time."

A sprig of holly lay by each plate, and nothing would do but each little Ruggles must leave his seat and have it pinned on by Carol, and as each course was served, one of them pleaded to take something to her. There was hurrying to and fro, I can assure you, for it is quite a difficult matter to serve a Christmas dinner on the third floor of a great city house; but if it had been necessary to carry every dish up a rope ladder the servants would gladly have done so. There were turkey and chicken, with delicious gravy and stuffing, and there were half a dozen vegetables, with cranberry jelly, and celery, and pickles; and as for the way these delicacies were served, the Ruggleses never forgot it as long as they lived.

Peter nudged Kitty, who sat next to him, and said, "Look, will yer, ev'ry feller's got his own partic'lar butter; I s'pose that's to show you can eat that 'n' no more. No, it ain't either, for that pig of a Peory's just gettin' another helpin'!"

"Yes," whispered Kitty, "an' the napkins is marked with big red letters! I wonder if that's so nobody'll nip 'em; an' oh, Peter, look at the pictures stickin' right on ter the dishes! Did yer ever?"

"The plums is all took out o' my cramb'ry sarse an' it's friz to a stiff jell!" whispered Peoria, in wild excitement.

"Hi—yah! I got a wish-bone!" sang Larry, regardless of Sarah Maud's frown; after which she asked to have his seat changed, giving as excuse that he "gen'ally set beside her, an' would feel strange"; the true reason being that she desired to kick him gently, under the table, whenever he passed what might be termed "the McGrill line."

"I declare to goodness," murmured Susan, on the other side, "there's so much to look at I can't scarcely eat nothin'!"

"Bet yer life I can!" said Peter, who had kept one servant busily employed ever since he sat down; for, luckily, no one was asked by Uncle Jack whether he would have a second helping, but the dishes were quietly passed under their noses, and not a single Ruggles refused anything that was offered him, even unto the seventh time.

Then, when Carol and Uncle Jack perceived that more turkey was a physical impossibility, the meats were taken off and the dessert was brought in—a dessert that would have frightened a strong man after such a dinner as had preceded it. Not so the Ruggleses—for a strong man is nothing to a small boy—and they kindled to the dessert as if the turkey had been a dream and six vegetables an optical delusion. There were plum-pudding, mince-pie, and ice-cream; and there were nuts, and raisins, and oranges. Kitty chose ice-cream, explaining that she knew it "by sight," though she "hadn't ever tasted none"; but all the rest took the entire variety, without any regard to consequences.

"My dear child," whispered Uncle Jack, as he took Carol an orange, "there is no doubt about the necessity of this feast, but I do advise you after this to have them twice a year, or quarterly perhaps, for the way these children eat is positively dangerous; I assure you I tremble for that terrible Peoria. I'm going to run races with her after dinner."

"Never mind," laughed Carol. "Let them have enough for once; it does my heart good to see them, and they shall come oftener next year."

The feast being over, the Ruggleses lay back in their chairs languidly, like little gorged boa-constrictors, and the table was cleared in a trice. Then a door opened into the next room, and there, in a corner facing Carol's bed, which had been wheeled as close as possible, stood the brilliantly lighted Christmas tree, glittering with gilded walnuts and tiny silver balloons, and wreathed with snowy chains of popcorn. The presents had been bought mostly with Carol's story-money, and were selected after long consultations with Mrs. Bird. Each girl had a blue knitted hood, and each boy a red crocheted comforter, all made by Mamma, Carol, and Elfrida. ("Because if you buy everything, it doesn't show so much love," said Carol.) Then every girl had a pretty plaid dress of a different color, and every boy a warm coat of the right size. Here the useful presents stopped, and they were quite enough; but Carol had pleaded to give them something "for fun." "I know they need the clothes," she had said, when they were talking over the matter just after Thanksgiving, "but they don't care much for them, after all. Now, Papa, won't you *please* let me go without part of my presents this year, and give me the money they would cost, to buy something to amuse the Ruggleses?"

"You can have both," said Mr. Bird, promptly. "Is there any need of my little girl's going without her own Christmas, I should like to know? Spend all the money you like."

"But that isn't the thing," objected Carol, nestling close to her father. "It wouldn't be mine. What is the use? Haven't I almost everything already, and am I not the happiest girl in the world this year, with Uncle Jack and Donald at home? You know very well it is more blessed to give than to receive; so why won't you let me do it? You never look half as happy when you are getting your presents as when you are giving us ours. Now, Papa, submit, or I shall have to be very firm and disagreeable with you!"

"Very well, your Highness, I surrender."

"That's a dear Papa! Now what were you going to give me? Confess!

"A bronze figure of Santa Claus; and in the 'little round belly that shakes when he laughs like a bowlful of jelly,' is a wonderful clock—oh, you would never give it up if you could see it!"

"Nonsense," laughed Carol; "as I never have to get up to breakfast, nor go to bed, nor catch trains, I think my old clock will do very well! Now, Mamma, what were you going to give me?"

"Oh, I hadn't decided. A few more books, and a gold thimble, and a smelling-bottle, and a music-box perhaps."

"Poor Carol," laughed the child, merrily, "she can afford to give up these lovely things, for there will still be Uncle Jack, and Donald, and Paul, and Hugh, and Uncle Rob, and Aunt Elsie, and a dozen other people to fill her Christmas stocking!"

So Carol had her way, as she generally did; but it was usually a good way, which was fortunate, under the circumstances; and Sarah Maud had a set of Miss Alcott's books, and Peter a modest silver watch, Cornelius a tool-chest, Clement a doghouse for his lame puppy, Larry a magnificent Noah's ark, and each of the younger girls a beautiful doll.

You can well believe that everybody was very merry and very thankful. All the family, from Mr. Bird down to the cook, said that they had never seen so much happiness in the space of three hours; but it had to end, as all things do. The candles flickered and went out, the tree was left alone with its gilded ornaments, and Mrs. Bird sent the children downstairs at half past eight, thinking that Carol looked tired.

"Now, my darling, you have done quite enough for one day," said Mrs. Bird, getting Carol into her little nightgown. "I'm afraid you will feel worse tomorrow, and that would be a sad ending to such a charming evening."

"Oh, wasn't it a lovely, lovely time," sighed Carol. "From first to last, everything was just right. I shall never forget Larry's face when he looked at the turkey; nor Peter's when he saw his watch; nor that sweet, sweet Kitty's smile when she kissed her dolly; nor the tears in poor, dull Sarah Maud's eyes when she thanked me for her books; nor—"

"But we mustn't talk any longer about it tonight," said Mrs. Bird, anxiously; "you are too tired, dear."

"I am not so very tired, Mamma. I have felt well all day; not a bit of pain anywhere. Perhaps this has done me good."

"Perhaps; I hope so. There was no noise or confusion; it was just a merry time. Now, may I close the door and leave you alone, dear? Papa and I will steal in softly by and by to see if you are all right; but I think you need to be very quiet."

"Oh, I'm willing to stay by myself; but I am not sleepy yet, and I am going to hear the music, you know."

"Yes, I have opened the window a little, and put the screen in front of it, so that you won't feel the air."

"Can I have the shutters open? and won't you turn my bed, please? This morning I woke ever so early, and one bright, beautiful star shone in that eastern window. I never noticed it before, and I thought of the Star in the East, that guided the wise men to the place where the baby Jesus was. Good-night, Mamma. Such a happy, happy day!"

"Good-night, my precious Christmas Carol—mother's blessed Christmas child."

"Bend your head a minute, mother dear," whispered Carol, calling her mother back. "Mamma, dear, I do think that we have kept Christ's birthday this time just as He would like it. Don't you?"

"I am sure of it," said Mrs. Bird, softly.

7

THE BIRDLING FLIES AWAY

The Ruggleses had finished a last romp in the library with Paul and Hugh, and Uncle Jack had taken them home and stayed a while to chat with Mrs. Ruggles, who opened the door for them, her face all aglow with excitement and delight. When Kitty and Clem showed her the oranges and nuts that they had kept for her, she astonished them by saying that at six o'clock Mrs. Bird had sent her in the finest dinner she had ever seen in her life; and not only that, but a piece of dress-goods that must have cost a dollar a yard if it cost a cent.

As Uncle Jack went down the rickety steps he looked back into the window for a last glimpse of the family, as the children gathered about their mother, showing their beautiful presents again and again—and then upward to a window in the great house yonder. "A little child shall lead them," he thought. "Well, if—if anything ever happens to Carol, I will take the Ruggleses under my wing."

"Softly, Uncle Jack," whispered the boys, as he walked into the library a while later. "We are listening to the music in the church. The choir has sung 'Carol, Brothers, Carol,' and now we think the organist is beginning to play 'My Ain Countree' for Carol."

"I hope she hears it," said Mrs. Bird; "but they are very late to-night, and I dare not speak to her lest she should be asleep. It is almost ten o'clock."

The boy soprano, clad in white surplice, stood in the organ loft. The light shone full upon his crown of fair hair, and his pale face, with its serious blue eyes, looked paler than usual. Perhaps it was something in the tender thrill of the voice, or in the sweet words, but there were tears in many eyes both in the church and in the great house next door.

I am far frae my hame,
I am weary aften whiles
For the langed-for hame-bringin',
An' my Faether's welcome smiles;
An' I'll ne'er be fu' content,
Until my e'en do see
The gowden gates o' heaven
In my ain countree.

The earth is decked wi' flow'rs,
Mony tinted, fresh an' gay,
An' the birdies warble blythely,
For my Faether made them sae;
But these sights an' these soun's
Will as naething be to me,
When I hear the angels singin'
In my ain countree.

Like a bairn to its mither,
A wee birdie to its nest,
I fain would be gangin' noo

Unto my Faether's breast;
For He gathers in His arms
Helpless, worthless lambs like me,
An' carries them Himsel'
To his ain countree.

There were tears in many eyes, but not in Carol's. The loving heart had quietly ceased to beat, and the "wee birdie" in the great house had flown to its "home nest." Carol had fallen asleep! But as to the song, I think perhaps, I cannot say, she heard it after all!

So sad an ending to a happy day! Perhaps—to those who were left; and yet Carol's mother, even in the freshness of her grief, was glad that her darling had slipped away on the loveliest day of her life, out of its glad content, into everlasting peace.

She was glad that she had gone as she had come, on the wings of song, when all the world was brimming over with joy; glad of every grateful smile, of every joyous burst of laughter, of every loving thought and word and deed the dear last day had brought.

Sadness reigned, it is true, in the little house behind the garden; and one day poor Sarah Maud, with a courage born of despair, threw on her hood and shawl, walked straight to a certain house a mile away, up the marble steps into good Dr. Bartol's office, falling at his feet as she cried, "Oh, sir, it was me an' our children that went to Miss Carol's last dinner-party, an' if we made her worse we can't never be happy again!" Then the kind old gentleman took her rough hand in his and told her to dry her tears, for neither she nor any of her flock had hastened Carol's flight; indeed, he said that had it not been for the strong hopes and wishes that filled her tired heart, she could not have stayed long enough to keep that last merry Christmas with her dear ones.

And so the old years, fraught with memories, die, one after another, and the new years, bright with hopes, are born to take their places; but Carol lives again in every chime of Christmas bells that peal glad tidings, and in every Christmas anthem sung by childish voices.

JOY

Sing hey for the chimney and roof-tree wide,
Sing hey for the walls and the floor,
For the warmth of the fire on the glowing hearth,
And the welcoming open door.
But most of all for the peace and goodwill
And the joy at our deep heart's core.

ELIZABETH GOUDGE

TAKE JOY!

FRA GIOVANNI
(c. 1513)

I salute you! There is nothing I can give you which you have not; but there is much, that, while I cannot give, you can take.

No heaven can come to us unless our hearts find rest in it today. *Take Heaven.*

No peace lies in the future which is not hidden in this present instant. *Take Peace.*

The gloom of the world is but a shadow; behind it, yet, within our reach, is joy. *Take Joy.*

And so, at this Christmas time, I greet you, with the prayer that for you, now and forever, the day breaks and the shadows flee away.

THE BELLS

EDGAR ALLAN POE
(1809–1849)

Hear the sledges with the bells—
    Silver bells!
What a world of merriment their melody foretells!
    How they tinkle, tinkle, tinkle,
        In the icy air of night!
    While the stars, that oversprinkle
    All the heavens, seem to twinkle
        With a crystalline delight
    Keeping time, time, time,
        In a sort of Runic rhyme,
To the tintinnabulation that so musically wells
    From the bells, bells, bells, bells,
        Bells, bells, bells—
From the jingling and the tinkling of the bells.

Christmas Every Day

WILLIAM DEAN HOWELLS
(1837–1920)

The little girl came into her papa's study, as she always did Saturday morning before breakfast, and asked for a story. He tried to beg off that morning, for he was very busy, but she would not let him. So he began:

"Well, once there was a little pig—"

She put her hand over his mouth and stopped him at the word. She said she had heard little pig stories till she was perfectly sick of them.

"Well, what kind of story *shall* I tell, then?"

"About Christmas. It's getting to be the season. It's past Thanksgiving already."

"It seems to me," argued her papa, "that I've told as often about Christmas as I have about little pigs."

"No difference! Christmas is more interesting."

"Well!" Her papa roused himself from his writing by a great effort. "Well, then, I'll tell you about the little girl that wanted it Christmas every day in the year. How would you like that?"

"First-rate!" said the little girl; and she nestled into a comfortable shape in his lap, ready for listening.

"Very well, then, this little pig,—Oh, what are you pounding me for?"

"Because you said little pig instead of little girl."

"I should like to know what's the difference between a little pig and a little girl that wanted it Christmas every day!"

"Papa," said the little girl, warningly, "if you don't go on, I'll *give* it to you!" And at this her papa darted off like lightning, and began to tell the story as fast as he could.

Well, once there was a little girl who liked Christmas so much that she wanted it to be Christmas every day in the year; and as soon as Thanksgiving was over she began to send postal cards to the old Christmas Fairy to ask if she mightn't have it. But the old Fairy never answered any of the postals; and, after a while, the little girl found out that the Fairy was pretty particular, and wouldn't notice anything but letters, not even correspondence cards in envelopes; but real letters on sheets of paper, and sealed outside with a monogram,—or your initial, anyway. So, then, she began to send her letters; and in about three weeks—or just the day before Christmas, it was—she got a letter from the Fairy, saying she might have it Christmas every day for a year, and then they would see about having it longer.

The little girl was a good deal excited already, preparing for the old-fashioned, once-a-year Christmas that was coming the next day, and perhaps the Fairy's promise didn't make such an impression on her as it would have made at some other time. She just resolved to keep it to herself, and surprise everybody with it as it kept coming true; and then it slipped out of her mind altogether.

She had a splendid Christmas. She went to bed early, so as to let Santa Claus have a chance at the stockings, and in the morning she was up the first of anybody and went and felt them, and found hers all lumpy with packages of candy, and oranges and grapes, and pocket-books and rubber balls and all kinds of small presents, and her big brother's with nothing but the tongs in them, and her young lady sister's with a new silk umbrella, and her papa's and mama's with potatoes and pieces of coal wrapped up in tissue paper, just as they always had every Christmas. Then she waited around till the rest of the family were up, and she was the first to burst into the library, when the doors were opened, and look at the large presents laid out on the library-table—books, and portfolios, and boxes of stationery, and breast-pins, and dolls, and little stoves, and dozens of handkerchiefs, and ink-stands, and skates, and snow-shovels, and photograph-frames, and little easels, and boxes of watercolors, and Turkish paste, and nougat, and candied cherries, and dolls' houses, and waterproofs,—and the big Christmas tree, lighted and standing in a wastebasket in the middle.

She had a splendid Christmas all day. She ate so much candy that she did not want any breakfast; and the whole forenoon the presents kept pouring in that the expressman had not had time to deliver the night before; and she went 'round giving the presents she had got for other people, and came home and ate turkey and cranberry for dinner, and plum-pudding and nuts and raisins and oranges and more candy, and then went out and coasted and came in with a stomachache, crying; and her papa said he would see if his house was turned into that sort of fool's paradise another year; and they had a light supper, and pretty early everybody went to bed cross.

Here the little girl pounded her papa in the back, again.

"Well, what now? Did I say pigs?"

"You made them *act* like pigs."

"Well, didn't they?"

"No matter; you oughtn't to put it into a story."

"Very well, then, I'll take it all out."

Her father went on:

The little girl slept very heavily, and she slept very late, but she was wakened at last by the other children dancing 'round her bed with their stockings full of presents in their hands.

"What is it?" said the little girl, and she rubbed her eyes and tried to rise up in bed.

"Christmas! Christmas! Christmas!" they all shouted, and waved their stockings.

"Nonsense! It was Christmas yesterday."

Her brothers and sisters just laughed. "We don't know about that. It's Christmas today, anyway. You come into the library and see."

Then all at once it flashed on the little girl that the Fairy was keeping her promise, and her year of Christmases was beginning. She was dreadfully sleepy, but she sprang up like a lark—a lark that had overeaten itself and gone to bed cross—and darted into the library. There it was again! Books, and portfolios, and boxes of stationery, and breast-pins—

"You needn't go over it all, Papa; I guess I can remember just what was there," said the little girl.

Well, and there was the Christmas tree blazing away, and the family picking out their presents, but looking pretty sleepy, and her father perfectly puzzled, and her mother ready to cry. "I'm sure I don't see how I'm to dispose of all these things," said her mother, and her father said it seemed to him they had had something just like it the day before, but he supposed he must have dreamed it. This struck the little girl as the best kind of a joke; and so she ate so much candy she didn't want any breakfast, and went 'round carrying presents, and had turkey and cranberry for dinner, and then went out and coasted, and came in with a—

"Papa!"
"Well, what now?"
"What did you promise, you forgetful thing?"
"Oh! oh, yes!"

Well, the next day, it was just the same thing over again, but everybody getting crosser; and at the end of a week's time so many people had lost their tempers that you could pick up lost tempers anywhere; they perfectly strewed the ground. Even when people tried to recover their tempers they usually got somebody else's, and it made the most dreadful mix.

The little girl began to get frightened, keeping the secret all to herself; she wanted to tell her mother, but she didn't dare to; and she was ashamed to ask the Fairy to take back her gift, it seemed ungrateful and ill-bred, and she thought she would try to stand it, but she hardly knew how she could, for a whole year. So it went on and on, and it was Christmas on St. Valentine's Day, and Washington's Birthday just the same as any day, and it didn't skip even the first of April, though everything was counterfeit that day, and that was some *little* relief.

After a while, coal and potatoes began to be awfully scarce, so many had been wrapped up in tissue paper to fool papas and mammas with. Turkeys got to be about a thousand dollars apiece—

"Papa!"
"Well, what?"
"You're beginning to fib."
"Well, *two* thousand, then."

And they got to passing off almost anything for turkeys—half-grown hummingbirds, and even rocs out of the "Arabian

Nights"—the real turkeys were so scarce. And cranberries—well, they asked a diamond apiece for cranberries. All the woods and orchards were cut down for Christmas trees, and where the woods and orchards used to be, it looked just like a stubblefield, with the stumps. After a while they had to make Christmas trees out of rags, and stuff them with bran, like old-fashioned dolls; but there were plenty of rags, because people got so poor, buying presents for one another, that they couldn't get any new clothes, and they just wore their old ones to tatters. They got so poor that everybody had to go to the poor-house, except the confectioners, and the fancy storekeepers, and the picture-booksellers, and the expressmen; and *they* all got so rich and proud that they would hardly wait upon a person when he came to buy; it was perfectly shameful!

Well, after it had gone on about three or four months, the little girl, whenever she came into the room in the morning and saw those great ugly lumpy stockings dangling at the fireplace, and the disgusting presents around everywhere, used to just sit down and burst out crying. In six months she was perfectly exhausted; she couldn't even cry any more; she just lay on the lounge and rolled her eyes and panted. About the beginning of October she took to sitting down on dolls, wherever she found them—French dolls, or any kind—she hated the sight of them so; and by Thanksgiving she was crazy, and just slammed her presents across the room.

But that time people didn't carry presents around nicely any more. They flung them over the fence, or through the window, or anything; and, instead of running their tongues out and taking great pains to write "For dear Papa," or "Mamma," or "Brother," or "Sister," or "Susie," or "Sammie," or "Billie," or "Bobby," or "Jimmie," or "Jennie," or whoever it was, and troubling to get the spelling right, and then signing their names, and "Xmas, 188-," they used to write in the gift-books, "Take it, you horrid old thing!" and then go and bang it against the front door. Nearly everybody had built barns to hold their presents, but pretty soon the barns overflowed, and then they used to let them lie out in the rain, or anywhere. Sometimes the police used to come and tell them to shovel their presents off the sidewalk, or they would arrest them.

"I thought you said everybody had gone to the poorhouse," interrupted the little girl.

"They did go, at first," said her papa; "but after a while the poorhouses got so full that they had to send the people back to their own houses. They tried to cry, when they got back, but they couldn't make the least sound."

"Why couldn't they?"

"Because they had lost their voices, saying 'Merry Christmas' so much. Did I tell you how it was on the Fourth of July?"

"No; how was it?" And the little girl nestled closer, in expectation of something uncommon.

Well, the night before, the boys stayed up to celebrate, as they always do, and fell asleep before twelve o'clock, as usual, expecting to be wakened by the bells and cannon. But it was nearly eight o'clock before the first boy in the United States woke up, and then he found out what the trouble was. As soon as he could get his clothes on, he ran out of the house and smashed a big cannon-torpedo down on the pavement; but it didn't make any more noise than a damp wad of paper, and, after he tried about twenty or thirty more, he began to pick them up and look at them. Every single torpedo was a big raisin! Then he just streaked upstairs, and examined his fire-crackers and toy-pistol and two-dollar collection of fireworks, and found that they were nothing but sugar and candy painted up to look like fireworks! Before ten o'clock, every boy in the United States found out that his Fourth of July things had turned into Christmas things; and then they just sat down and cried—they were so mad. There are about twenty million boys in the United States, and so you can imagine what a noise they made. Some men got together before night, with a little powder that hadn't turned into purple sugar yet, and they said they would fire off *one* cannon, anyway. But the cannon burst into a thousand pieces, for it was nothing but rock-candy, and some of the men nearly got killed. The Fourth of July orations all turned into Christmas carols, and when anybody tried to read the Declaration, instead of saying, "When in the course of human events it becomes necessary," he was sure to sing, "God Rest Ye, Merry Gentlemen." It was awful.

The little girl drew a deep sigh of satisfaction.

"And how was it at Thanksgiving?" she asked.

Her papa hesitated. "Well, I'm almost afraid to tell you. I'm afraid you'll think it's wicked."

"Well, tell, anyway," said the little girl.

Well, before Thanksgiving came, it had leaked out who had caused all these Christmases. The little girl had suffered so much that she had talked about it in her sleep; and after that, hardly anybody would play with her. People just perfectly despised her, because if it had not been for her greediness, it wouldn't have happened; and now, when it came Thanksgiving, and she wanted them to go to church, and have squash-pie and turkey, and show their gratitude, they said that all the turkeys had been eaten up for her old Christmas dinners, and if she would stop the Christmases, they would see about the gratitude. Wasn't it dreadful? And the very next day the little girl began to send letters to the Christmas Fairy, and then telegrams, to stop it. But it didn't do any good; and then she got to calling at the Fairy's house, but the girl that came to the door always said "Not at home," or "Engaged," or "At dinner," or something like that; and so it went on till it came to the old once-a-year Christmas Eve. The little girl fell asleep, and when she woke up in the morning—

"She found it was all nothing but a dream," suggested the little girl.

"No, indeed!" said her papa. "It was all every bit true!"

"Well, what *did* she find out then?"

"Why, that it wasn't Christmas at last, and wasn't ever going to be, any more. Now it's time for breakfast."

The little girl held her papa fast around the neck.

"You sha'n't go if you're going to leave it *so!*"

"How do you want it left?"

"Christmas once a year."

"All right," said her papa; and he went on again.

Well, there was the greatest rejoicing all over the country, and it extended clear up into Canada. The people met together everywhere, and kissed and cried for joy. The city carts went around and gathered up all the candy and raisins and nuts, and dumped them into the river; and it made the fish perfectly sick; and the whole United States, as far out as Alaska, was one blaze of bonfires, where the children were burning up their gift-books and presents. They had the greatest *time!*

The little girl went to thank the old Fairy because she had stopped its being Christmas, and she said she hoped she would keep her promise, and see that Christmas never, never came again. Then the Fairy frowned, and asked her if she was sure she knew what she meant; and the little girl asked her, why not? and the old Fairy said that now she was behaving just as greedily as ever, and she'd better look out. This made the little girl think it all over carefully again, and she said she would be willing to have it Christmas about once in a thousand years; and then she said a hundred, and then she said ten, and at last she got down to one. Then the Fairy said that was the good old way that had pleased people ever since Christmas began, and she was agreed. Then the little girl said, "What're your shoes made of?" And the Fairy said, "Leather." And the little girl said, "Bargain's done forever," and skipped off, and hippity-hopped the whole way home, she was so glad.

"How will that do?" asked the papa.

"First-rate!" said the little girl; but she hated to have the story stop, and was rather sober. However, her mamma put her head in at the door, and asked her papa:

"Are you never coming to breakfast? What have you been telling that child?"

"Oh, just a moral tale."

The little girl caught him around the neck again.

"*We* know! Don't you tell *what,* Papa! Don't you tell *what!*"

GLORIOUS NEWS

LUKE 2:8-20

There were some shepherds living in the same part of the country, keeping guard throughout the night over their flock in the open fields. Suddenly an angel of the Lord stood before them, the splendor of the Lord blazed around them, and they were terror-stricken. But the angel said to them,

"Do not be afraid! Listen, I bring you glorious news of great joy which is for all the people. This very day, in David's town, a Savior has been born for you. He is Christ, the Lord. Let this prove it to you: you will find a baby wrapped up and lying in a manger."

And in a flash there appeared with the angel a vast host of the armies of Heaven, praising God, saying,

"Glory to God in the highest Heaven! Peace upon earth among men of goodwill!"

When the angels left them and went back into Heaven, the shepherds said to each other,

"Now let us go straight to Bethlehem and see this thing which the Lord has made known to us."

So they went as fast as they could and they found Mary and Joseph—and the babe lying in the manger. And when they had seen this sight, they told everybody what had been said to them about the little child. And all those who heard them were amazed at what the shepherds said. . . . And the shepherds went back to work, glorifying and praising God for everything that they had heard and seen.

CHRISTMAS

GEORGE HERBERT
(1593–1633)

The shepherds sing; and shall I silent be?
My God, no hymne for thee?
My soul's a shepherd too; a flock it feeds
Of thoughts, and words, and deeds.
The pasture is thy word: the streams, thy grace
Enriching all the place.
Shepherd and flock shall sing, and all my powers
Out-sing the day-light houres.
Then we will chide the sunne for letting night
Take up his place and right:
We sing one common Lord; wherefore he should
Himself the candle hold.
I will go searching, till I finde a sunne
Shall stay, till we have done;
A willing shiner, that shall shine as gladly,
As frost-nipt sunnes look sadly.
Then we will sing, and shine all our own day,
And one another pay:
His beams shall cheer my breast, and both so twine,
Till ev'n his beams sing, and my musick shine.

CHRISTMAS AT ORCHARD HOUSE

from *Little Women*

LOUISA MAY ALCOTT
(1832–1888)

"Christmas won't be Christmas without any presents," grumbled Jo, lying on the rug.

"It's so dreadful to be poor!" sighed Meg, looking down at her old dress.

"I don't think it's fair for some girls to have plenty of pretty things, and other girls nothing at all," added little Amy, with an injured sniff.

"We've got Father and Mother, and each other," said Beth contentedly from her corner.

The four young faces on which the firelight shone brightened at the cheerful words, but darkened again as Jo said sadly, "We haven't got Father, and shall not have him for a long time." She didn't say "perhaps never," but each silently added it, thinking of Father far away, where the fighting was.

Nobody spoke for a minute; then Meg said in an altered tone, "You know the reason Mother proposed not having any presents this Christmas was because it is going to be a hard winter for everyone; and she thinks we ought not to spend money for pleasure, when our men are suffering so in the army. We can't do much, but we can make our little sacrifices, and ought to do it gladly. But I am afraid I don't." And Meg shook her head, as she thought regretfully of all the pretty things she wanted.

"But I don't think the little we should spend would do any good. We've each got a dollar, and the army wouldn't be much helped by our giving that. I agree not to expect anything from Mother or you, but I do want to buy *Undine and Sintram* for myself. I've wanted it *so* long," said Jo, who was a bookworm.

"I planned to spend mine in new music," said Beth, with a little sigh, which no one heard but the hearth brush and kettle holder.

"I shall get a nice box of Faber's drawing pencils. I really need them," said Amy decidedly.

"Mother didn't say anything about our money, and she won't wish us to give up everything. Let's each buy what we want, and have a little fun. I'm sure we work hard enough to earn it," cried Jo, examining the heels of her shoes in a gentlemanly manner.

"I know *I* do—teaching those tiresome children nearly all day, when I'm longing to enjoy myself at home," began Meg, in the complaining tone again.

"You don't have half such a hard time as I do," said Jo. "How would you like to be shut up for hours with a nervous, fussy old lady, who keeps you trotting, is never satisfied, and worries you till you're ready to fly out the window or cry?"

"It's naughty to fret, but I do think washing dishes and keeping things tidy is the worst work in the world. It makes me cross, and my hands get so stiff, I can't practice well at all." And Beth looked at her rough hands with a sigh that any one could hear that time.

"I don't believe any of you suffer as I do," cried Amy, "for you don't have to go to school with impertinent girls, who plague you if you don't know your lessons, and laugh at your dresses, and label your father if he isn't rich, and insult you when your nose isn't nice."

"If you mean *libel,* I'd say so, and not talk about *labels,* as if Papa was a pickle bottle," advised Jo, laughing.

"I know what I mean, and you needn't be *statirical* about it. It's proper to use good words, and improve your *vocabilary,"* returned Amy, with dignity.

"Don't peck at one another, children. Don't you wish we had the money Papa lost when we were little, Jo? Dear me! How happy and good we'd be, if we had no worries!" said Meg, who could remember better times.

"You said the other day you thought we were a deal happier than the King children, for they were fighting and fretting all the time, in spite of their money."

"So I did, Beth. Well, I think we are; for, though we do have to work, we make fun for ourselves, and are a pretty jolly set, as Jo would say."

"Jo does use such slang words!" observed Amy, with a reproving look at the long figure stretched on the rug. Jo immediately sat up, put her hands in her pockets, and began to whistle.

"Don't, Jo, it's so boyish!"

"That's why I do it."

"I detest rude, unladylike girls!"

"I hate affected, niminy-piminy chits!"

" 'Birds in their little nests agree,' " sang Beth, the peacemaker, with such a funny face that both sharp voices softened to a laugh, and the "pecking" ended for that time.

"Really, girls, you are both to be blamed," said Meg, beginning to lecture in her elder-sisterly fashion. "You are old enough to leave off boyish tricks, and to behave better, Josephine. It didn't matter so much when you were a little girl, but now you are so tall, and turn up your hair, you should remember that you are a young lady."

"I'm not! And if turning up my hair makes me one, I'll wear it in two tails till I'm twenty," cried Jo, pulling off her net, and shaking down a chestnut mane. "I hate to think I've got to grow up, and be Miss March, and wear long gowns, and look as prim as a China aster! It's bad enough to be a girl, anyway, when I like boy's games and work and manners! I can't get over my disappointment in not being a boy. And it's worse than ever now, for I'm dying to go and fight with Papa, and I can only stay home and knit, like a poky old woman!" And Jo shook the blue army sock till the needles rattled like castanets, and her ball bounded across the room.

"Poor Jo! It's too bad, but it can't be helped. So you must try to be contented with making your name boyish, and playing brother to us girls," said Beth, stroking the rough head with a hand that all the dishwashing and dusting in the world could not make ungentle in its touch.

"As for you, Amy," continued Meg, "you are altogether too particular and prim. Your airs are funny now, but you'll grow up an affected little goose, if you don't take care. I like your nice manners and refined ways of speaking, when you don't try to be elegant. But your absurd words are as bad as Jo's slang."

"If Jo is a tomboy and Amy a goose, what am I, please?" asked Beth, ready to share the lecture.

"You're a dear, and nothing else," answered Meg warmly, and no one contradicted her, for the "Mouse" was the pet of the family.

As young readers like to know "how people look," we will take this moment to give them a little sketch of the four sisters, who sat knitting away in the twilight, while the December snow fell quietly without, and the fire crackled cheerfully within. It was a comfortable old room, though the carpet was faded and the furniture very plain, for a good picture or two hung on the walls, books filled the recesses, chrysanthemums and Christmas roses bloomed in the windows, and a pleasant atmosphere of home peace pervaded it.

Margaret, the eldest of the four, was sixteen, and very pretty, being plump and fair, with large eyes, plenty of soft, brown hair, a sweet mouth, and white hands, of which she was rather vain. Fifteen-year-old Jo was very tall, thin, and brown, and reminded one of a colt, for she never seemed to know what to do with her long limbs, which were very much in her way. She had a decided mouth, a comical nose, and sharp, gray eyes, which appeared to see everything, and were by turns fierce, funny, or thoughtful. Her long, thick hair was her one beauty, but it was usually bundled into a net, to be out of her way. Round shoulders had Jo, big hands and feet, a flyaway look to her clothes, and the uncomfortable appearance of a girl who was rapidly shooting up into a woman and didn't like it. Elizabeth, or Beth, as everyone called her, was a rosy, smooth-haired, bright-eyed girl of thirteen, with a shy manner, a timid voice, and a peaceful expression which was seldom disturbed. Her father called her "Little Tranquillity," and the name suited her excellently, for she seemed to live in a happy world of her own, only venturing out to meet the few whom she trusted and loved. Amy, though the youngest, was a most important person, in her own opinion at least. A regular snow maiden, with blue eyes, and yellow hair curling on her shoulders, pale and slender, and always carrying herself like a young lady mindful of her manners. What the characters of the four sisters were we will leave to be found out.

The clock struck six and, having swept up the hearth, Beth put a pair of slippers down to warm. Somehow the sight of the old shoes had a good effect upon the girls, for Mother was coming, and everyone brightened to welcome her. Meg stopped lecturing, and lighted the lamp, Amy got out of the easy chair without being asked, and Jo forgot how tired she was as she sat up to hold the slippers nearer to the blaze.

"They are quite worn out. Marmee must have a new pair."

"I thought I'd get her some with my dollar," said Beth.

"No, I shall!" cried Amy.

"I'm the oldest," began Meg, but Jo cut in with a decided—

"I'm the man of the family now Papa is away, and *I* shall provide the slippers, for he told me to take special care of Mother while he was gone."

"I'll tell you what we'll do," said Beth, "let's each get her something for Christmas, and not get anything for ourselves."

"That's like you, dear! What will we get?" exclaimed Jo.

Everyone thought soberly for a minute, then Meg announced, as if the idea was suggested by the sight of her own pretty hands, "I shall give her a nice pair of gloves."

"Army shoes, best to be had," cried Jo.

"Some handkerchiefs, all hemmed," said Beth.

"I'll get a little bottle of cologne. She likes it, and it won't cost much, so I'll have some left to buy my pencils," added Amy.

"How will we give the things?" asked Meg.

"Put them on the table, and bring her in and see her open the bundles. Don't you remember how we used to do on our birthdays?" answered Jo.

"I used to be *so* frightened when it was my turn to sit in the chair with the crown on, and see you all come marching round to give the presents, with a kiss. I liked the things and the kisses, but it was dreadful to have you sit looking at me while I opened the bundles," said Beth, who was toasting her face and the bread for tea at the same time.

"Let Marmee think we are getting things for ourselves, and then surprise her. We must go shopping tomorrow afternoon, Meg. There is so much to do about the play for Christmas night," said Jo, marching up and down, with her hands behind her back and her nose in the air.

"I don't mean to act any more after this time. I'm getting too old for such things," observed Meg, who was as much a child as ever about "dressing-up" frolics.

"You won't stop, I know, as long as you can trail round in a white gown with your hair down, and wear gold-paper jewelry. You are the best actress we've got, and there'll be an end of everything if you quit the boards," said Jo. "We ought to rehearse tonight. Come here, Amy, and do the fainting scene, for you are as stiff as a poker in that."

"I can't help it. I never saw anyone faint, and I don't choose to make myself all black and blue, tumbling flat as you do. If I can go down easily, I'll drop; if I can't, I shall fall into a chair and be graceful. I don't care if Hugo does come at me with a pistol," returned Amy, who was not gifted with dramatic power, but was chosen because she was small enough to be borne out shrieking by the villain of the piece.

"Do it this way. Clasp your hands so, and stagger across the room, crying frantically, 'Roderigo! Save me! Save me!' " and away went Jo, with a melodramatic scream which was truly thrilling.

Amy followed, but she poked her hands out stiffly before her, and jerked herself along as if she went by machinery, and her "Ow!" was more suggestive of pins being run into her than of fear and anguish. Jo gave a despairing groan, and Meg laughed outright, while Beth let her bread burn as she watched the fun with interest.

"It's no use! Do the best you can when the time comes, and if the audience laughs, don't blame me. Come on, Meg."

Then things went smoothly, for Don Pedro defied the world in a speech of two pages without a single break; Hagar, the witch, chanted an awful incantation over her kettleful of simmering toads, with weird effect; Roderigo rent his chains asunder manfully, and

Hugo died in agonies of remorse and arsenic, with a wild "Ha! Ha!"

"It's the best we've had yet," said Meg, as the dead villain sat up and rubbed his elbows.

"I don't see how you can write and act such splendid things, Jo. You're a regular Shakespeare!" exclaimed Beth, who firmly believed that her sisters were gifted with wonderful genius in all things.

"Not quite," replied Jo modestly. "I do think *The Witch's Curse, an Operatic Tragedy* is rather a nice thing, but I'd like to try *Macbeth,* if we only had a trapdoor for Banquo. I always wanted to do the killing part. 'Is that a dagger that I see before me?' " muttered Jo, rolling her eyes and clutching at the air, as she had seen a famous tragedian do.

"No, it's the toasting fork, with Mother's shoe on it instead of the bread. Beth's stage-struck!" cried Meg, and the rehearsal ended in a general burst of laughter.

"Glad to find you so merry, my girls," said a cheery voice at the door, and actors and audience turned to welcome a tall, motherly lady with a "can-I-help-you" look about her which was truly delightful. She was not elegantly dressed, but a noble-looking woman, and the girls thought the gray cloak and unfashionable bonnet covered the most splendid mother in the world.

"Well, dearies, how have you got on today? There was so much to do, getting the boxes ready to go tomorrow, that I didn't come home to dinner. Has anyone called, Beth? How is your cold, Meg? Jo, you look tired to death. Come and kiss me, baby."

While making these maternal inquiries Mrs. March got her wet things off, her warm slippers on, and sitting down in the easy chair, drew Amy to her lap, preparing to enjoy the happiest hour of her busy day. The girls flew about, trying to make things comfortable, each in her own way. Meg arranged the tea table, Jo brought wood and set chairs, dropping, over-turning, and clattering everything she touched. Beth trotted to and fro between parlor and kitchen, quiet and busy, while Amy gave directions to everyone, as she sat with her hands folded.

As they gathered about the table, Mrs. March said, with a particularly happy face, "I've got a treat for you after supper."

A quick, bright smile went round like a streak of sunshine. Beth clapped her hands, regardless of the biscuit she held, and Jo tossed up her napkin, crying, "A letter! A letter! Three cheers for Father!"

"Yes, a nice long letter. He is well, and thinks he shall get through the cold season better than we feared. He sends all sorts of loving wishes for Christmas, and an especial message to you girls," said Mrs. March, patting her pocket as if she had got a treasure there.

"Hurry and get done! Don't stop to quirk your little finger and simper over your plate, Amy," cried Jo, choking on her tea and dropping her bread, butter side down, on the carpet in her haste to get at the treat.

Beth ate no more, but crept away to sit in her shadowy corner and brood over the delight to come, till the others were ready.

"I think it was so splendid in Father to go as a chaplain when he was too old to be drafted, and not strong enough for a soldier," said Meg warmly.

"Don't I wish I could go as a drummer, a *vivan*—what's its name? Or a nurse, so I could be near him and help him," exclaimed Jo, with a groan.

"It must be very disagreeable to sleep in a tent, and eat all sorts of bad-tasting things, and drink out of a tin mug," sighed Amy.

"When will he come home, Marmee?" asked Beth, with a little quiver in her voice.

"Not for many months, dear, unless he is sick. He will stay and do his work faithfully as long as he can, and we won't ask for him back a minute sooner than he can be spared. Now come and hear the letter."

They all drew to the fire, Mother in the big chair with Beth at her feet, Meg and Amy perched on either arm of the chair, and Jo leaning on the back, where no one would see any sign of emotion if the letter should happen to be touching. Very few letters were written in those hard times that were not touching, especially those which fathers sent home. In this one little was said of the hardships endured, the dangers faced, or the homesickness conquered. It was a cheerful, hopeful letter, full of lively descriptions of camp life, marches, and military news, and only at the end did the writer's heart overflow with fatherly love and longing for the little girls at home.

"Give them all my dear love and a kiss. Tell them I think of them by day, pray for them by night, and find my best comfort in their affection at all times. A year seems very long to wait before I see them, but remind them that while we wait we may all work, so that these hard days need not be wasted. I know they will remember all I said to them, that they will be loving children to you, will do their duty faithfully, fight their bosom enemies bravely, and conquer themselves so beautifully that when I come back to them I may be fonder and prouder than ever of my little women."

Everybody sniffed when they came to that part; Jo wasn't ashamed of the great tear that dropped off the end of her nose, and Amy never minded the rumpling of her curls as she hid her face on her mother's shoulder and sobbed out, "I *am* a selfish girl! But I'll truly try to be better, so he mayn't be disappointed in me by-and-by."

"We all will!" cried Meg."I think too much of my looks and hate to work, but won't any more, if I can help it."

"I'll try and be what he loves to call me, 'a little woman,' and not be rough and wild, but do my duty here instead of wanting to be somewhere else," said Jo, thinking that keeping her temper at home was a much harder task than facing a rebel or two down South.

Beth said nothing, but wiped away her tears with the blue army sock and began to knit with all her might, losing no time in doing the duty that lay nearest her, while she resolved in her quiet little soul to be all that Father hoped to find her when the year brought round the happy coming home.

Mrs. March broke the silence that followed Jo's words, by saying in her cheery voice, "Do you remember how you used to play Pilgrim's Progress when you were little things? Nothing delighted you more than to have me tie my piece-bags on your backs for burdens, give you hats and sticks and rolls of paper, and let you travel through the house from the cellar, which was the City of Destruction, up, up, to the housetop, where you had all the lovely things you could collect to make a Celestial City."

"What fun it was, especially going by the lions, fighting Apollyon, and passing through the Valley where the hobgoblins were!" said Jo.

"I liked the place where the bundles fell off and tumbled downstairs," said Meg.

"My favorite part was when we came out on the flat roof where our flowers and arbors and pretty things were, and all stood and sung for joy up there in the sunshine," said Beth, smiling, as if that pleasant moment had come back to her.

"I don't remember much about it, except that I was afraid of the cellar and the dark entry, and always liked the cake and milk we had up at the top. If I wasn't too old for such things, I'd rather like to play it over again," said Amy, who began to talk of renouncing childish things at the mature age of twelve.

"We never are too old for this, my dear, because it is a play we are playing all the time in one way or another. Our burdens are here, our road is before us, and the longing for goodness and happiness is the guide that leads us through many troubles and mistakes to the peace which is a true Celestial City. Now, my little pilgrims, suppose you begin again, not in play, but in earnest, and see how far on you can get before Father comes home."

"Really, Mother? Where are our bundles?" asked Amy, who was a very literal young lady.

"Each of you told what your burden was just now, except Beth. I rather think she hasn't got any," said her mother.

"Yes, I have. Mine is dishes and dusters, and envying girls with nice pianos, and being afraid of people."

Beth's bundle was such a funny one that everybody wanted to laugh, but nobody did, for it would have hurt her feelings very much.

"Let us do it," said Meg thoughtfully. "It is only another name for trying to be good, and the story may help us, for though we do want to be good, it's hard work and we forget, and don't do our best."

"We were in the Slough of Despond tonight, and Mother came and pulled us out as Help did in the book. We ought to have our roll of directions, like Christian. What shall we do about that?" asked Jo, delighted with the fancy which lent a little romance to the very dull task of doing her duty.

"Look under your pillows Christmas morning, and you will find your guidebook," replied Mrs. March.

They talked over the new plan while old Hannah cleared the table, then out came the four little workbaskets, and the needles flew as the girls made sheets for Aunt March. It was uninteresting sewing, but tonight no one grumbled. They adopted Jo's plan of dividing the long seams into four parts, and calling the quarters Europe, Asia, Africa, and America, and in that way got on capitally, especially when they talked about the different countries as they stitched their way through them.

At nine they stopped work, and sang, as usual, before they went to bed. No one but Beth could get much music out of the old piano, but she had a way of softly touching the yellow keys and making a pleasant accompaniment to the simple songs they sang. Meg had a voice like a flute, and she and her mother led the little choir. Amy chirped like a cricket, and Jo wandered through the airs at her own sweet will, always coming out at the wrong place with a croak or a quaver that spoiled the most pensive tune. They had always done this from the time they could lisp "Crinkle, crinkle, 'ittle 'tar," and it had become a household custom, for the mother was a born singer. The first sound in the morning was her voice as she went about the house singing like a lark, and the last sound at night was the same cheery sound, for the girls never grew too old for that familiar lullaby.

Jo was the first to wake in the gray dawn of Christmas morning. No stockings hung at the fireplace, and for a moment she felt as much disappointed as she did long ago, when her little sock fell down because it was so crammed with goodies. Then she remembered her mother's promise and, slipping her hand under her pillow, drew out a little crimson-covered book. She knew it very well, for it was that beautiful old story of the best life ever lived, and Jo felt that it was a true guidebook for any pilgrim going on a long journey. She woke Meg with a "Merry Christmas," and bade her see what was under her pillow. A green-covered book appeared, with the same picture inside, and a few words written by their mother, which made their one present very precious in their eyes. Presently Beth and Amy woke to rummage and find their little books also—one dove-colored, the other blue—and all sat looking at and talking about them, while the east grew rosy with the coming day.

In spite of her small vanities, Margaret had a sweet and pious nature, which unconsciously influenced her sisters, especially Jo, who loved her very tenderly, and obeyed her because her advice was so gently given.

"Girls," said Meg seriously, looking from the tumbled head beside her to the two little nightcapped ones in the room beyond, "Mother wants us to read and love and mind these books, and we must begin at once. We used to be faithful about it, but since Father went away and all this war trouble unsettled us, we have neglected many things. You can do as you please, but *I* shall keep my book on the table here and read a little every morning as soon as I wake, for I know it will do me good and help me through the day."

Then she opened her new book and began to read. Jo put her arm round her and, leaning cheek to cheek, read also, with the quiet expression so seldom seen on her restless face.

"How good Meg is! Come, Amy, let's do as they do. I'll help you with the hard words, and they'll explain things if we don't understand," whispered Beth, very much impressed by the pretty books and her sisters' example.

"I'm glad mine is blue," said Amy. And then the rooms were very still while the pages were softly turned, and the winter sunshine crept in to touch the bright heads and serious faces with a Christmas greeting.

"Where is Mother?" asked Meg, as she and Jo ran down to thank her for their gifts, half an hour later.

"Goodness only knows. Some poor creeter came a-beggin', and your ma went straight off to see what was needed. There never *was* such a woman for givin' away vittles and drink, clothes and firin'," replied Hannah, who had lived with the family since Meg was born, and was considered by them all more as a friend than a servant.

"She will be back soon, I think, so fry your cakes, and have everything ready," said Meg, looking over the presents which were collected in a basket and kept under the sofa, ready to be produced at the proper time. "Why, where is Amy's bottle of cologne?" she added, as the little flask did not appear.

"She took it out a minute ago, and went off with it to put a ribbon on it, or some such notion," replied Jo, dancing about the room to take the first stiffness off the new army slippers.

"How nice my handkerchiefs look, don't they? Hannah washed and ironed them for me, and I marked them all myself," said Beth, looking proudly at the somewhat uneven letters which had cost her such labor.

"Bless the child! She's gone and put 'Mother' on them instead of 'M. March.' How funny!" cried Jo, taking up one.

"Isn't it right? I thought it was better to do it so, because Meg's initials are M. M., and I don't want anyone to use these but Marmee," said Beth, looking troubled.

"It's all right, dear, and a very pretty idea—quite sensible, too, for no one can ever mistake now. It will please her very much, I know," said Meg, with a frown for Jo and a smile for Beth.

"There's Mother. Hide the basket, quick!" cried Jo, as a door slammed and steps sounded in the hall.

Amy came in hastily, and looked rather abashed when she saw her sisters all waiting for her.

"Where have you been, and what are you hiding behind you?" asked Meg, surprised to see, by her hood and cloak, that lazy Amy had been out so early.

"Don't laugh at me, Jo! I didn't mean anyone should know till the time came. I only meant to change the little bottle for a big one, and I gave *all* my money to get it, and I'm truly trying not to be selfish any more."

As she spoke, Amy showed the handsome flask which replaced the cheap one, and looked so earnest and humble in her little effort to forget herself that Meg hugged her on the spot, and Jo pronounced her "a trump," while Beth ran to the window, and picked her finest rose to ornament the stately bottle.

"You see I felt ashamed of my present, after reading and talking about being good this morning, so I ran round the corner and changed it the minute I was up: and I'm *so* glad, for mine is the handsomest now."

Another bang of the street door sent the basket under the sofa, and the girls to the table, eager for breakfast.

"Merry Christmas, Marmee! Many of them! Thank you for our books; we read some, and mean to every day," they cried in chorus.

"Merry Christmas, little daughters! I'm glad you began at once, and hope you will keep on. But I want to say one word before we sit down. Not far away from here lies a poor woman with a little newborn baby. Six children are huddled into one bed to keep from freezing, for they have no fire. There is nothing to eat over there, and the oldest boy came to tell me they were suffering hunger and cold. My girls, will you give them your breakfast as a Christmas present?"

They were all unusually hungry, having waited nearly an hour, and for a minute no one spoke—only a minute, for Jo exclaimed impetuously, "I'm so glad you came before we began!"

"May I go and help carry the things to the poor little children?" asked Beth eagerly.

"*I* shall take the cream and the muffins," added Amy, heroically giving up the articles she most liked.

Meg was already covering the buckwheats, and piling the bread into one big plate.

"I thought you'd do it," said Mrs. March, smiling as if satisfied. "You shall all go and help me, and when we come back we will have bread and milk for breakfast, and make it up at dinnertime."

They were soon ready, and the procession set out. Fortunately it was early, and they went through back streets, so few people saw them, and no one laughed at the queer party.

A poor, bare, miserable room it was, with broken windows, no fire, ragged bedclothes, a sick mother, wailing baby, and a group of pale, hungry children cuddled under one old quilt, trying to keep warm.

How the big eyes stared and the blue lips smiled as the girls went in!

"Ach, mein Gott! It is good angels come to us!" said the poor woman, crying for joy.

"Funny angels in hoods and mittens," said Jo, and set them laughing.

In a few minutes it really did seem as if kind spirits had been at work there. Hannah, who had carried wood, made a fire, and stopped up the broken panes with old hats and her own cloak. Mrs. March gave the mother tea and gruel, and comforted her with promises of help, while she dressed the little baby as tenderly as if it had been her own. The girls meantime spread the table, set the children round the fire, and fed them like so many hungry birds—laughing, talking, and trying to understand the funny broken English.

"Das ist gut!" "Die Engel-kinder!" cried the poor things as they ate and warmed their purple hands at the comfortable blaze.

The girls had never been called angel children before, and thought it very agreeable, especially Jo, who had been considered a "Sancho" ever since she was born. That was a very happy breakfast, though they didn't get any of it; and when they went away, leaving comfort behind, I think there were not in all the city four merrier people than the hungry little girls who gave away their breakfasts and contented themselves with bread and milk on Christmas morning.

"That's loving our neighbor better than ourselves, and I like it," said Meg, as they set out their presents while their mother was upstairs collecting clothes for the poor Hummels.

Not a very splendid show, but there was a great deal of love done up in the few little bundles, and the tall vase of red roses, white chrysanthemums, and trailing vines, which stood in the middle, gave quite an elegant air to the table.

"She's coming! Strike up, Beth! Open the door, Amy! Three cheers for Marmee!" cried Jo, prancing about while Meg went to conduct Mother to the seat of honor.

Beth played her gayest march, Amy threw open the door, and Meg enacted escort with great dignity. Mrs. March was both surprised and touched, and smiled with her eyes full as she examined her presents and read the little notes which accompanied them. The slippers went on at once, a new handkerchief was slipped into her pocket, well scented with Amy's cologne, the rose was fastened in her bosom, and the nice gloves were pronounced a "perfect fit."

There was a good deal of laughing and kissing and explaining, in the simple, loving fashion which makes these home festivals so pleasant at the time, and so sweet to remember long afterward.

What Can I Give Him?

CHRISTINA G. ROSSETTI
(1830–1894)

What can I give Him,
Poor as I am?
If I were a shepherd
I would bring a lamb;
If I were a wise man
I would do my part—
Yet what I can, I give Him,
Give my heart.

THE LAMB

WILLIAM BLAKE
(1757–1827)

Little Lamb, who made thee?
Dost thou know who made thee?
Gave thee life, and bid thee feed
By the stream and o'er the mead;
Gave thee clothing of delight,
Softest clothing, wooly, bright;
Gave thee such a tender voice,
Making all the vales rejoice!
Little Lamb, who made thee?
Dost thou know who made thee?

Little Lamb, I'll tell thee,
Little Lamb, I'll tell thee:
He is called by thy name,
For he calls himself a Lamb.
He is meek, and he is mild;
He became a little child.
I a child, and thou a lamb,
We are called by his name.
Little Lamb, God bless thee!
Little Lamb, God bless thee!

THE ELM SCHOOL CHRISTMAS PLAY

NELSON BENTLEY
(1918–)

My acting career began when I was nine,
In the Elm School Christmas Play, which took place
In the Big Room; the fifth through eighth grades met
There, beneath pictures of *The Lone Wolf* and George
Washington. The previous weekend I had climbed in
Through an unlatched window, with Willie Esch,
To release a trapped sparrow. This took some tall
Explaining to Sam Burke, the baker, who stood waiting
Amid frozen sandburs as I clambered out,
Sparrow in hand. I remember the swings clanking

In the wintry gale, and the whinny of Lena Booker's
Spavined horse, looking over the broken wire
Fence. Sam was on his way to the Elm General Store,
And listened suspiciously, his platter of jelly
Doughnuts steaming in sparsely falling snow.
By the night of the play, the audience had to battle
Through drifts, in their Model T's and Reos, or by foot.
As the curtain cheesecloth, hung on a wire clothesline,

Opened, I wandered on stage, yawned, curled up in
A chair and went to sleep. The play was my dream.

I maintained a beatific face, though peeking,
While Gooseneck Gaffney, as Gabriel, gave the prologue,
After which entered Buck St. Clair, fresh from his
Skunk trapping, as Joseph; Rosie Zink as
The Virgin Mary, holding her doll, Clara Bow;
And Rube Whitehead, as the donkey. Above them,
Stage rear, stood, precariously balanced on a high
Stool, Horseneck Gaffney, Star of the Nativity,
With an enormous flashlight. Then came the Heavenly
Chorus, consisting of Wilhelmina Hawley,

C. C. Hogan, who had spit out his Peachy Scrap
Just before entering (he'd been chewing since he was five),
August Card, who resembled a grizzly bear
From the rear, Stinkymouse Steiner, Lloyd Trinka,
Lena and Myrtle Booker, and Eddie Cunningham.
When they'd finished "Hark, the Herald Angels Sing,"
There was a loud clumping sound and the Three Wise Men
Appeared: Willie Esch, Billy Wolfram and Karl Stapp,
Wearing oriental rugs. Simultaneously,
Stage left, Stanley Hayes led the three shepherds;

The other two were Walter Sharrow and Ty Place,
Who had dislocated my shoulder two years before.
Stanley was working his way through grade school
In a White Star gas station. He was carrying
A shepherd's crook eight feet long; it resembled
A hook I'd seen used in vaudeville to drag off
Unsuccessful acts. All three shepherds wore

Flour sacks from Sam Burke's bakery. They kept
Their eyes fixed on Horseneck, the guiding star,
While Willie presented frankincense and myrrh,

And Rube gave an occasional soft hee-haw.
I noticed Walter and Ty holding either end
Of a long strip of General Store wrapping paper
On which were drawn in crayon twelve skinny sheep,
Resembling a band of collie dogs, ears dragging
On the ground. Finally the entire cast
Sang "Oh Little Town of Bethlehem" while snowflakes
Fell thickly past the big windows looking out
On Booker's pasture, and all filed offstage,
From Willie Esch to Rube Whitehead. I yawned,

Rose, stretched, and started off for bed, as Stanley
Hayes, who had hastily turned into Santa Claus,
Tiptoed onstage, his huge suit hanging in folds,
Looking a little like a skinned bear, his beard
Made from a mop, his galoshes unbuckled;
Followed by Willie Esch as Blitzen, looking more
Like a giraffe than a reindeer. They leaped about,
Flinging popcorn bags and leading one more song,
By audience and actors; hoofs and galoshes thumped,
And "Jingle Bells" floated out over fields and barns.

SOMEHOW NOT ONLY FOR CHRISTMAS

JOHN GREENLEAF WHITTIER
(1807–1892)

Somehow not only for Christmas
    But all the long year through,
The joy that you give to others
    Is the joy that comes back to you.

And the more you spend in blessing
    The poor and lonely and sad,
The more of your heart's possessing
    Returns to make you glad.

A PRAYER FOR CHRISTMAS MORNING

HENRY VAN DYKE
(1852–1933)

The day of joy returns, Father in heaven, and crowns another year with peace and good will.

Help us rightly to remember the birth of Jesus, that we may share in the song of the angels, the gladness of the shepherds, and the worship of the wise men.

May the Christmas morning make us happy to be thy children, and the Christmas evening bring us to our bed with grateful thoughts, forgiving and forgiven, for Jesus' sake. Amen

HOPE

The wolf will live with the lamb,
The leopard will lie down with the goat,
The calf and the lion and the yearling together;
And a little child will lead them.

THE BOOK OF ISAIAH

THE VOICE OF THE CHRIST-CHILD

PHILLIPS BROOKS
(1835–1893)

The earth has grown old with its burden of care,
But at Christmas it always is young,
The heart of the jewel burns lustrous and fair,
And its soul full of music breaks forth on the air,
When the song of the angels is sung.

It is coming, old earth, it is coming tonight,
On the snowflakes which cover thy sod,
The feet of the Christ-child fall gently and white,
And the voice of the Christ-child tells out with delight
That mankind are the children of God.

On the sad and the lonely, the wretched and poor,
That voice of the Christ-child shall fall;
And to every blind wanderer opens the door

Of a hope which he dared not to dream of before,
With a sunshine of welcome for all.

The feet of the humblest may walk in the field
Where the feet of the holiest have trod,
This, this is the marvel to mortals revealed,
When the silvery trumpets of Christmas have pealed,
That mankind are the children of God.

CHRISTMAS CAROL

HENRY WADSWORTH LONGFELLOW
(1807–1882)

When Christ was born in Bethlehem,
'Twas night, but seemed the noon of day;
    The stars, whose light
    Was pure and bright,
    Shone with unwavering ray;
But one, one glorious star
Guided the Eastern Magi from afar.

Then peace was spread throughout the land;
The lion fed beside the tender lamb;
    And with the kid,
    To pasture led,
    The spotted leopard fed;
In peace, the calf and bear,
The wolf and lamb reposed together there.

As shepherds watched their flocks by night,
An angel, brighter than the sun's own light,

Appeared in air,
And gently said,
Fear not,—be not afraid,
For lo! beneath your eyes,
Earth has become a smiling paradise.

AWAY IN A MANGER

JON PETERSON
(1972–)

"Now please stand and turn in your hymnals to hymn number 45, 'O Little Town of Bethlehem,'" Pastor Lundin said. As the congregation pulled the hymnals from the racks and flipped through the pages, he read the first lines:

O little town of Bethlehem
How still we see thee lie;
Above thy deep and dreamless sleep
The silent stars go by.

He raised his hand, pinched his index finger and thumb together, as if holding a baton, and, when his hand came down, the small congregation began to sing, accompanied by his wife Mary on the warbling Hammond electric organ.

The pageant's gone off without a hitch; I can't believe it, he thought as his swaying arm led them into the end of the first verse. In his twenty-four years at Our Savior's Lutheran Church in Milton, Minnesota, he could remember but a handful of children's pageants that hadn't ended with a candle stand being knocked over, a keep-away game with the baby Jesus, or a crying shepherd running off the stage to his nervous mother.

Yet in the dark streets shineth
The everlasting light
The hopes and fears of all the years
Are met in thee tonight.

As the second verse ended, Pastor Lundin noticed that several members of the church had turned their heads. A bright light had caught their eyes. Something was happening on the front lawn. Eventually everyone but Mrs. Lundin, whose back was turned to the windows, stopped singing. Earl Swanson left his back-pew seat and went outside the church into the snow. He burst back in before the door had swung shut, stood at the back of the sanctuary and shouted, "Pastor! The manger's on fire!"

The church emptied almost before Earl could get out of the way. Pastor Lundin went out through the side exit and saw his congregation standing ankle-deep in the snow, staring blankly at the inferno. The church's new crèche, the one they had bought just weeks before, was engulfed in flames.

Before this Christmas, Our Savior's had used the same crèche for thirty-five years—the one Oscar Knutson had built and the rest of the congregation had slowly added on to in the late 1950s. The old nativity scene wasn't all that fancy—each figure had come from someone's basement or attic. Mary and Joseph were dusty mannequins with bathrobes thrown over them to hide the fact that they had no legs. Oscar's daughter, Emily, had provided the Baby Jesus when she gave the church one of her baby dolls—one with its arms outstretched and a bright look in its glass eyes that told her that it would make a perfect Baby Jesus. The only problem with the doll was that Emily had fallen down the stairs once when she was four while cradling it in her arms. The doll took the only serious bruising of the fall, losing its hands.

Over the next few years, different members of Our Savior's had added their touches to the Christmas scene. Irene English and Oscar's wife, Vivian, donated most of the bathrobes and dish towels for the figures' clothing. The Hendricks donated four additional mannequins to be Shepherds. Helen Larrimer made two sheep out of sawhorses, lots of cotton, and a good deal of imagination. Somehow, the church ended up with six Wise Men, all bearing gifts of gold, since no one was quite sure what frankincense and myrrh looked like. To accompany the Wise Men and Shepherds, the youth group rolled out snowmen every winter, dressing them to look like Abraham Lincoln, Frosty, and President Eisenhower.

In 1962 Mayor Ernie Fenton asked Oscar if he would donate the crèche to be used in front of Milton's town hall. With the congregation's permission, he hauled the whole collection down the street in the back of his pickup. The manger scene at town hall became a source of pride for Our Savior's. Members of the congregation would often detour their routes home to take a look at their accomplishment. The nativity scene also became a favorite site of caroling, Christmas night walks, and snowball fights.

One year the manger scene saved the Christmas pageant at Our Savior's when Susie Olson forgot to bring her doll to be Baby Jesus. Playing the part of Mary, it was her responsibility to bring the Baby. Minutes before the pageant began, her father Alvin ran the six blocks to the town hall to get the doll from the crèche. For years after that, his wife Sarah teased him about running to the government to find Jesus.

In 1977, when Vice President Mondale came to Milton and spoke outside the town hall at Christmas, he remarked that the crèche was a "very nice touch" to the Christmas decorations around the town. The comment was lost by nearly everyone in attendance, but not to the members of Our Savior's, and certainly not to Oscar Knutson, who wrote down what the vice president said, just so he wouldn't forget it.

Mary and Joseph, the six Wise Men, the presidential snowmen, the Shepherds, and their sawhorse sheep had stared down at the Baby Jesus with his outstretched, handless arms in front of town hall every Christmas until this year, when the city council voted, 5-to-4, that the scene depicted an "historic, religious event on public property that pertains to one specific faith and violates the Constitutional right of the separation of church and state." The council ordered the church to take back their crèche and, if they wanted it displayed, to display it only on church property.

After thirty-five years of standing out in Minnesota winters, the figures had begun to show the abuse of weather. They had all gone through numerous robe changes and face paintings but were now really falling apart. Earl Swanson was the first in the congregation to suggest that maybe it was time to retire the old nativity scene. He had seen some churches in the Twin Cities that had those new plastic figures with lights inside them. They were pretty durable and, as they glowed, could be seen from all over. "Maybe it's time for Our Savior's to move into the 1990s," he said.

Oscar Knutson wasn't convinced. He argued that the mannequins needed another coat of paint and some new robes. "It really wouldn't be all that hard," he insisted. "I could have them ready to go by Christmas, good as new." But new was 1958, Earl told him. It didn't matter if Oscar could get the figures looking lifelike if their lives still looked like 1958. The congregation wasn't convinced, until Earl agreed to pay half the cost of the new crèche.

The holy plastic family was purchased in early November, unwrapped, and set up two weeks before Christmas. Mary, Joseph, the three Wise Men, the two Shepherds, and the smiling Baby with his arms and fists frozen in mid-squirm were lit up every Sunday and Wednesday night. Their glowing bodies proclaimed to the whole town the coming of a hip Savior.

On the night of the Christmas pageant, Earl wanted to show the more skeptical members of the congregation that purchasing the new crèche was worth the money they had spent. For the last few nights, the glowing characters had told the story of Christ coming into the world, but tonight Earl wanted them to shout it. He wanted the whole town to be drawn to Our Savior's by a Christmas light not unlike the ancient star that had led the wise men to the stable two thousand years ago.

He began by taking the 75-watt bulbs out of the bases of the figures and replacing them with 150-watt floodlight bulbs. If the people were out of their homes tonight, he figured that a little bright outdoor advertising at the Lutheran church might bring them in. He saw his improvements as evangelistic work—calling the folk from the country hills with bright lights just as the heavenly hosts of angels had on that first Christmas. It would be quite a sight.

Earl was more than successful. The figures, huddled underneath the wooden stable backdrop, blazed with light. As they entered the church, members of the congregation congratulated Earl. "Spectacular," they said. "We could see it even as we left the house." "It's the most incredible thing we've ever seen."

The eight figures stood glowing outside the church throughout the pageant. But by the time the host of child cherubs had waddled on stage to sing "Hark the Herald Angels Sing" inside the church, Joseph was beginning to feel quite warm outside. The four 150-watt bulbs Earl had screwed into his feet were beginning to make his head melt.

While the pageant was ending, Mary's face began to droop, her chin slowly resting and then running down her chest. Then Joseph's shoulders sagged, and a moment later the towel wrapped around his plastic head ignited as it sank and rolled off into the straw-filled manger, which immediately caught fire. In an amazing reenactment of the Spirit descending on the twelve Apostles at Pentecost, the hay above the Shepherd's heads burst into flames and alerted the congregation inside that there was anything but a silent night going on out on the front lawn.

By the time everyone had emptied out of the church and realized what was happening, there was little left to do but stand and watch the fire burn itself out in the snow. Some of the more skeptical members who had opposed buying a new crèche all along remarked that the fire had been sent from heaven as a judgment on the wandering church. Others mumbled something about Catholics and the town council. Pastor Lundin looked around for Oscar Knutson but couldn't find him.

Minutes later, after the scene had been reduced to a pool of bubbling black plastic in the burned lawn, the congregation noticed Oscar and four other men emerging from the side entrance carrying mannequins in their arms. Fifteen minutes later Joseph and Mary, six Wise Men, two Shepherds, and a couple of sawhorse sheep were staring down at a crippled Baby. The sheep were for the most part cotton-less and the Baby lay naked, his broken arms outstretched. All in all, thought Pastor Lundin, it was a pretty pitiful little sight.

He looked down the street, past Woolworth's and Hoiggard Motors and saw town hall, standing dark and heavy in the cold snow. As he turned his head to look back, he was startled to hear his congregation, standing around the crèche, singing "O Little Town of Bethlehem" on the verse where they had left off:

How silently, how silently
The wondrous gift is giv'n;
So God imparts to human hearts
The blessings of His heav'n.

Pastor Lundin smiled and, putting his hand on Oscar's shoulder, began to sing.

A CHRISTMAS CAROL

G. K. CHESTERTON
(1874–1936)

The Christ-child lay on Mary's lap,
His hair was like a light.
(O weary, weary were the world,
But here is all aright.)

The Christ-child lay on Mary's breast,
His hair was like a star,
(O stern and cunning are the kings,
But here the true hearts are.)

The Christ-child lay on Mary's heart,
His hair was like a fire.
(O weary, weary is the world,
But here the world's desire.)

The Christ-child stood at Mary's knee,
His hair was like a crown,
And all the flowers looked up at Him,
And all the stars looked down.

A CRADLE SONG

WILLIAM BLAKE
(1757–1827)

Sleep, sleep, happy child,
All creation slept and smil'd;
Sleep, sleep, happy sleep,
While o'er thee thy mother weep.

Sweet babe, in thy face
Holy image I can trace.
Sweet babe, once like thee,
Thy maker lay and wept for me,

Wept for me, for thee, for all,
When he was an infant small.
Thou his image ever see,
Heavenly face that smiles on thee,

Smiles on thee, on me, on all;
Who became an infant small.
Infant smiles are his own smiles;
Heaven and earth to peace beguiles.

A NIGHT THE STARS DANCED FOR JOY

BOB HARTMAN
(1955–)

The old shepherd, the shepherd's wife, and the shepherd boy lay on their backs on top of the hill. Their hands were folded behind their heads, and their feet stretched out in three directions like points on a compass. Their day's work was done. Their sheep had dropped off to sleep. And they had run out of things to say.

So they just lay there on top of that hill and stared lazily into the night sky.

It was a clear night. There were no clouds for shy stars to hide behind. And the bolder stars? For some reason, they seemed to be shining more proudly than even the old shepherd could remember.

Suddenly, what must have been the boldest star of all came rushing across the sky, dancing from one horizon to the other and showing off its sparkling serpent's tail.

"Shooting star," said the boy dreamily. "Make a wish."

The old shepherd and his wife said nothing. They were too old for games and too tired, tonight, even to say so.

But they were not too old for wishing.

The old shepherd fixed his eyes on a cluster of stars that looked like a great bear. And he thought about the cluster of scars on his leg—jagged reminders of a battle he'd fought with a real bear long ago. A battle to save his sheep. He had been young and strong then. He'd won that battle.

There were other scars, too, mapped out like a hundred roads across his back. Souvenirs of his battles with that Great Bear, Rome. The land of Israel belonged to his people, not to the Roman invaders who were devouring it with their tyranny and taxes. So why should he bow politely to Roman soldiers and surrender his sheep for their banquets? Greedy tyrants. Uniformed thieves. That's what they were—the lot of them. And even their claw-sharp whips would not change his mind.

And so, even though he said nothing, the old shepherd made a wish. He wished for someone to save him. From violence. From greed. From bears.

The shepherd's wife had her eyes shut. This was the hardest time of the day for her. The time when there was nothing to do but try to fall asleep. The time when the wind always carried voices back to her. Her voice and her mother's. Angry, bitter voices. Voices hurling words that hurt. Words she wished she'd never spoken. Words she couldn't take back now, because her mother was dead. And there was no chance to say she was sorry.

And so, even though she said nothing, the shepherd's wife silently wished for peace, for an end to those bitter voices on the wind.

The shepherd boy grew tired of waiting.

"All right," he said finally, "*I'll* make a wish then. I wish . . . I wish . . . I wish something interesting would happen for a change.

Something exciting. I'm tired of just sitting on this hill night after night. I want something to laugh about. To sing and dance about."

The old shepherd turned to look at his wife.

The shepherd's wife opened her eyes and shook her head.

But before either of them could lecture their son about being satisfied with what he had, something happened. Something that suggested the shepherd boy just might get his wish.

Like tiny white buds blossoming into gold flowers, the stars began to swell and spread, until their edges bled together and the sky was filled with a glowing blanket of light. And then that blanket of light began to shrink and gather itself into a brilliant, blinding ball that hung above the shepherds and left the rest of the sky black and empty.

Wide-eyed and slack-jawed, the shepherds dared not move. The wind had stopped. And the shepherds lay glued to the hillside, staring into that light. They watched it slowly change again. Shining rays stretched into arms. Legs kicked out like white beams. And a glowing face blinked bright and burning. The light sprouted wings. It took the shape of an angel. And it spoke.

"Don't be afraid," the angel said. "But sing and dance for joy! I have good news for you. Today, in Bethlehem, your Savior was born—the Special One whom God promised to send you. Here's the proof: if you go to Bethlehem, you will find the baby wrapped in cloths and lying in a feed trough."

The shepherds were still too shocked to speak. But that didn't keep them from thinking.

Don't be afraid? thought the old shepherd. *He's got to be kidding.*

A baby in a feed trough? thought the shepherd's wife. *Why, even our own son got better treatment than that.*

Sing and dance for joy? thought the shepherd boy. *Now that's more like it!*

And, as if in answer to the boy's thought, the angel threw his arms and legs wide, like the first step in some heavenly jig. But instead, he flung himself—could it be?—into a thousand different pieces of light, pieces that scattered themselves across the dark blue of the night and landed where the stars had been. Pieces that turned into angels themselves, singing a song that the shepherds had never heard before, to a tune that had been humming in their heads forever.

"Glory to God in the highest!" the angels sang. "And peace on earth to all."

Some plucked at lyres. Some blew trumpets. Some beat drums. Some banged cymbals. There were dancers, as well—spinning and whirling, larking and leaping across the face of the midnight moon.

Finally, when the music could get no louder, when the singers could sing no stronger, when the dancers could leap no higher, when the shepherds' mouths and eyes could open no further, everything came to a stop.

As quickly as the angels had come, they were gone. The sky was silent and filled once more with twinkling stars. The shepherds lay there for a moment, blinking and rubbing their eyes.

At last the old shepherd struggled to his feet. "Well," he said, "looks like we'd better find this baby."

The shepherd's wife pulled herself up, shook the grass off her robe and ran her fingers absently through her hair.

The shepherd boy leaped eagerly to his feet and shouted "Hooray!"

When they got to Bethlehem, things were just as the angel had said. A husband and a young mother. And a baby in a feed trough.

A family much like the shepherd's, in fact. Was it possible, the old man wondered, for one so small, so poor, so ordinary, to be the Savior? The Promised One?

Then he told the young mother about the angels. And that's when he knew. It was the look in her eyes. The look that said, "How wonderful!" but also, "I'm not surprised." There was something special going on here. The angels knew it. The mother knew it. And now the shepherd and his family knew it, too.

"Well," said the boy as they made their way back to the hill, "my wish came true. Too bad you didn't make a wish."

The old shepherd said nothing. But he ran one finger gently along his scars. Was he imagining things, or were they smaller now?

The shepherd's wife said nothing. She was listening. There were no bitter voices on the wind now. There were songs—heaven songs—and the cry of a newborn child.

"Glory to God in the highest!" she shouted suddenly.

"And peace to everyone on earth!" the old shepherd shouted back.

Then the shepherd boy shouted, too—"Hooray!"—and danced like an angel for joy.

BORN TO RAISE THE SONS OF EARTH

MARK NOLL
(1946–)

I am busy, Jesus,
ever faster screeching round and round—
you lie calmly in the manger,
Joseph's patient voice the only sound.

I am selfish, Jesus,
grasping, pulling inward, curved in tight—
you stoop lower, ever lower,
mixing spittle for a poor man's sight.

I am sated, Jesus,
stuffed so full I've almost lost my breath—
you are rasping, breathing labored,
stumbling naked, famished to your death.

I am tired, Jesus,
numb and finished, callous and distressed—
you stand wounded, weeping, dying,
quickened; calling, "Come to me and rest."

PAPERWHITES

SANNA ANDERSON BAKER
(1949–)

I

We celebrated well:
took from attic boxes marked "Christmas"
coils of garlands,
wired them to railings, windowsills, doorcasings,
then punctuated with red velvet bows.
We bore into the house the ten-foot tree
radiating cold and the pungence of pine,
wove into its green
star lights
scattering, evenly we hoped,
forty purple satin hearts,
a host of angels
and apples by the dozen.

On Christmas Eve
both sides of family gathered
and in the beatific candle glow
tasted the sweetness
of the little Lord Jesus asleep on the hay.
We celebrated the Word made Flesh

and for a time joy bloomed wild.
But we cannot hold at bay too long
the thought of Flesh—
all flesh—
torn.

II

The carload of poinsettias,
at first Santa Barbara lush,
are looking leggy.
My eye tires of the assertiveness of red,
the optimism of green.
It craves faded greys and browns
against a ground of white.
And so we pack away the hearts and lights,
re-coil the greens,
and through the undressed window watch
the children on their fluorescent sleds and saucers
take the hill
or on their Christmas skates
circumnavigate the reed-clogged swamp.

I am ready for ordinary time,
for bare white window sills
and surfaces swept clean,
for the more modest hope of paperwhite narcissus.
For weeks the bulbs have sat on my windowsill
    anchored in a bed of stones.
I watch them
as I slice oranges, dredge chicken, wash dishes.
The host of tiny white flowers
folded, confined

swell
stretching green-veined skin
until it is translucent.

I think about the bulbs I've planted through the years—
snowdrops, crocus, hyacinth, daffodil, tulip.
About the iris rhizomes,
the tuberous roots of peonies dug from my
    mother's garden,
the fleshy roots of daylilies harvested from the
    vacant lot,
remnant of some settler's garden gone to seed.
I think about the bulbs I planted this year in
    late November.
Cold was coming, and I planted until after dark.
The yard light helped some,
but mostly I had to feel,
setting the pointed ends up.
My hands were muddy and numb.
That night it froze hard.

III

And today the children went back to school,
the oldest bemoaning the way her bangs looked,
the middle one fiercely wrestling her school bag
    and cello
into the neighbor's station wagon,
the youngest sad for the demands life makes
when there is sledding and the swamp is frozen.
I waved them off, put the dog out, and poured another
    cup of coffee.
From the kitchen table I look beyond the weathered deck

to the empty yard, and beyond it
to the woods against a leaden sky.
The house would not sell well in winter.
People would find the view bleak at best.
They could not imagine the glorious improbabilities—
May apples
giant Jack-in-the-pulpits
wild ginger
trillium
lily of the valley
violets
the drift of Virginia bluebells about the oak
the waves of yellow daffodils—
hidden in rhizomes, roots, bulbs.

The first of the paperwhites has burst.
In medieval times people kept *memento mori*.
A skull on a desk, perhaps.
I do not know Latin, how to turn
memento mori to its opposite
but I keep paperwhite narcissus
on my windowsill
in January.

LOVE CAME DOWN AT CHRISTMAS

CHRISTINA G. ROSSETTI
(1830–1894)

Love came down at Christmas,
    Love all lovely, Love Divine;
Love was born at Christmas,
    Star and angels gave the sign.

Love shall be our token,
    Love be yours and love be mine,
Love to God and all men,
    Love for plea and gift and sign.